BURNT OFFERINGS

On November 13, 1992, firemen attacked the blaze inside the Coulson family home in the Spring Branch section of Houston. They kicked in the front door and entered the smoky gloom.

Nothing could have prepared them for the horror they found.

In the back bedroom, a large man, probably over six feet tall and 200 pounds, lay face down on the bed, his hands tied behind him. A woman was only two feet from the man, lying on her side, curled up like a baby in a womb. In another bedroom were two more bodies: a rather large woman and a slight man. She was lying on the bed and he was curled on the floor. A young woman was curled up on the floor in the front bedroom.

Their bodies were burned almost beyond recognition, and each member of the Coulson family had been bound with zip cords. White trash compactor bags, secured with duct tape, shrouded the victims' heads. Duct tape locked their legs together, too, and sealed their mouths and noses. Their eyes had been cooked by the intense heat, their ears and noses charred. One of the women had been six months pregnant.

GRUESOME REAL LIFE EVENTS FROM PINNACLE TRUE CRIME

ASHES TO ASHES

Lyn Riddle

Pinnacle Books
Kensington Publishing Corp.

http://www.pinnaclebooks.com

Some names have been changed to protect the privacy of individuals connected to this story.

PINNACLE BOOKS are published by

Kensington Publishing Corp.
850 Third Avenue
New York, NY 10022

Pinnacle and the P logo Reg. U.S. Pat. & TM Off.

First Printing: May, 1997

Printed in the United States of America
10 9 8 7 6 5 4 3 2 1

For Mary

and mothers like her who center their children's lives with abiding love

Earth to earth, ashes to ashes, dust to dust, the Lord bless her and keep her, the Lord makes his face to shine upon her and be gracious unto her, the Lord lift up his countenance upon her and give her peace.

—*Book of Common Prayers*

ACKNOWLEDGMENTS

The one source of joy to come from writing Mary Coulson's story has been getting acquainted with her friends and family. Maggi Tucker and Barbara Dove, her longtime friends, provided insight and interesting anecdotes to liven the tale. Peter Coulson, Otis' brother, dusted off documents, photographs and letters, some three decades old.

Officers of the court offered immeasurable aid. Thanks especially to prosecutor Chuck Rosenthal, court reporter Christine Neal, and past and present officers of the Houston Police Department, Dale Achetee, Terry Ross, Brad Rudolph and Billy Belk.

Much gratitude goes to my agent, Frank Weimann, who took a chance on an unknown newspaper reporter with a good story, and my editor Karen Haas, who made the storytelling better.

I simply could not have completed this task without the understanding of my family, my husband Don and our children Josh, Lauren and Colin. They endured a dusty house and a surly wife and mom as the lonely process of writing went on for weeks on end.

Finally, heartfelt thanks to Linda Mary Danner Payne, who trusted me enough to tell her beloved aunt's story. The process sometimes felt painful, but getting to know Mary Coulson through her journals and letters, her friends and acquaintances, added immeasurably to my life.

AUTHOR'S NOTE

At 54, Mary Coulson had come to a crossroads in her life. Her children were grown and, for the most part, living independently. It was time, finally, to think of herself. Maybe she'd finish the children's book about an adventurous hippopotamus she sketched out years earlier in a small brown notebook. Certainly she would continue writing religious music with her friend Maggi Tucker. In fact, their newest anthem was to be published soon. The class she taught with an assistant rector at St. Francis Episcopal Church was going well and her parents seemed to have reached something of a plateau in their delicate advanced years.

Then on a seemingly uneventful November day, Mary and her family received a most unwelcome visitor. In the way that fate can sometimes be cruelly ironic, it was someone she had greeted with open arms twenty years earlier. Mary Coulson's story holds little joy but offers a lesson for us all. With indefatigable spirit, Mary Coulson took in children unwanted and gave them the love they craved. She made them her own. While expecting an Ozzie and Harriet family, Mary Coulson acquired instead something more akin to those featured in Pat Conroy novels: unceasingly anguished.

An adoptive mother, about the same age as Mary Coulson once said, "Adoptive parents adopt other people's pain." Women of their age thought their primary role was to be a mother. If they could bear no children of their own, they would take in someone else's.

Mary Coulson's story is not an indictment of adoption per se. It simply raises questions. Are some children too damaged by parental abuse and neglect to fit into a traditional home? Does society and, most especially the nation's extensive network of social service agencies, owe families like the Coulsons hands-on and frequent help in dealing with troubled youngsters?

Mary Coulson never gave up. She believed love would conquer all. Like most mothers, Mary blamed herself for her children's failings. If she were here today, she would probably wonder just what she could have done differently to make things turn out right. The answer is simple: not a thing, Mary. Not a thing.

—Lyn Riddle
Simpsonville, South Carolina
December 16, 1996

PART I:
The Investigation

Chapter One

Crawling beneath dense smoke, firefighter Bill Lobins did not know for sure that bodies were in the house until he reached out in the darkness and felt a woman's foot.

The 911 call to Houston emergency dispatchers at a quarter past six on November 13, 1992, Friday the 13th, said only that a house in the Spring Branch section was on fire. A neighbor, Mike Gherman, had placed the call. Recuperating from knee surgery, the aircraft mechanic stepped outside his own modest home that evening, hoping the unseasonably warm weather had cooled enough to have a fire in his fireplace. Smoke filled the sky. He hobbled around to his backyard and saw smoke billowing from the side of the Coulson home. After calling the fire department, he quickly stashed his dog in the laundry room, grabbed his garden hose and doused the side of the Coulsons' brick house. He had been their neighbor for sixteen years, ever since he moved to Houston from New Jersey to work with Northrop. Gherman prized friendly neighbors like Otis and Mary. They didn't socialize, but frequently talked across carefully cultivated yards.

That afternoon, he had gone to the store about 3:00 P.M. Returning a couple of hours later, he had noticed four cars in his neighbors' driveway. A usual Friday for the Coulsons, he had thought. Their grown kids were visiting for their weekly get-together.

Within minutes of his call, Engine Company No. 49 arrived. They cut off the gas with the special scanning tool firefighters carry, disconnected the main switchbox and called the power company to cut the line and yank out the meter. Gherman screamed, "There's people in there!" as firemen attacked the blaze.

About that time, Engine Company No. 5 rolled up to the front of the house. Lobins, a fifteen-year veteran of the Houston Fire Department, was the acting captain that day. He saw the cars in the drive and guessed people were inside. It would be his job to perform the search and rescue as the other crew extinguished the blaze. Attired in bunker gear—a heavy suit and mask that can withstand fire—Lobins and the first lineman headed for the front door. The thick and burly lineman tried to turn the locked doorknob, and then with one strong kick, broke the front door down. Smoke banked from the ceiling to the floor, and Lobins could see fire flickering in the left side of the house, where Company 49 worked feverishly. He noticed the garage was located to the left of the house and instinctively headed to the right, where he assumed the bedrooms were located. He smelled the distinctive odor of gasoline.

His flashlight illuminating the way, Lobins could see only about two feet ahead. He ended up in a bedroom at the end of the house. Groping in the darkness, he felt a foot. Then he saw a brassiere and knew he had touched a woman. Positioning his light, he saw her feet were together and her hands were together. Then he saw they were tied. He grabbed hold of her leg and her shoulder, fumbling for life, but she was stiff.

A firefighter in another bedroom shouted, "There's a body in here."

Lobins made his way to that bedroom and saw a woman with a cast on her leg.

"Do you want to start CPR?" the firefighter asked.

"No," Lobins responded. "They're gone. Leave them alone. Don't move them."

This was no ordinary house fire. This was now a crime scene.

After telling the chief about the bodies, Lobins went back into the rear bedroom. The firefighters began to check for extension of fire, a term they use for the way fire gets into walls, ceilings, attics, any place where it can hide, smoldering and ready to erupt anew. They tore a hole in the roof to let the toxic and explosive fumes seep out. The smoke in the back bedroom cleared some as firefighters opened windows. Lobins saw a large man, probably over six feet tall and 200 pounds, lying facedown on the bed, his hands tied behind him. He looked like a stiff tree toppled by a fierce wind. The woman he had seen earlier was only two feet from the man, lying on her side, curled up like a baby in a womb. White plastic bags covered their heads and silver-colored duct tape encircled their necks like a brace.

Lobins stepped through the house and into another

bedroom at the opposite side, built inside the garage. There were two more bodies there, a rather large woman and a slight man. She was lying on the bed, he was curled on the floor.

The bodies were so badly burned, investigators couldn't tell who was who. Each member of the family had been bound with zip cords, the quarter-inch-thick nylon bands electricians use to tie wires together permanently. The harder a zip cord is pulled apart, the tighter it gets. Hands tied with zip cords would never be free. White trash compactor bags, secured with duct tape, shrouded the victims' heads. Duct tape locked their legs together, too, and sealed their mouths and noses.

Chapter Two

Dale Achetee and Terry Ross held a distinctive status among Houston police homicide detectives. In their nine years riding together, they had come to be known as the king and queen of the multiples, police slang for murders involving more than one person.

"If the Iraqis decided to blow up the airport, we'd be the first one out," Ross often said. The detectives had already cleared five quadruples and who knows how many triples and doubles. They made a good team. Wiry and thin, Achetee had an intense air about him. Yet he had the accepting way of a preacher, helping him to win the confidence of witnesses and suspects alike. Ross had a photographic memory. Precise and ordered, she could map out a crime scene with such precision, it could be faithfully reconstructed years later from her notes alone.

Sometime after 7:00 P.M. on November 13, 1992, Lieutenant Kunkle strode into their cubicle in the central station in downtown Houston.

"Y'all saddle up," he said. "I got five burned bodies in a house."

"Lieutenant, you got to be kidding. Don't kid me," Achetee responded.

"I'm not," the lieutenant declared. "I've got five burned bodies."

"Holy shit," Achetee said, grimacing toward his partner and grabbing his gear: a briefcase he rarely took out of the patrol car and a flashlight.

The detectives drove the ten miles to the Spring Branch section of the city in near silence, listening to police radio prattle. The house on Westview was a medium-sized ranch in a nice but unimposing section. Fire engines, pumpers and police cars blocked the street, a major thoroughfare lined with decades-old oaks and houses built within the last thirty years.

A "For Sale" sign lay tipped on its side, and several cars covered the drive. Smoke seeped through holes in the roof. The Houston Fire Department had rigged floodlights to stands inside the house, and Achetee could see eerie shadows of firefighters moving around inside, dousing a few smoldering spots. Giant fans blew smoke through the windows. Neighbors kept a quiet vigil outside.

Achetee and Ross knew only that the home belonged to a Mr. and Mrs. Otis Coulson, who were probably in their sixties. Neighbors confided that a daughter in her early twenties lived with them. A Toyota Corolla parked in the driveway had already been traced to Richard Wentworth, the Coulsons' son-in-law. The detectives presumed the fifth victim to be his wife Robin, the Coulsons' twenty-five-year-old daughter.

Stepping inside, the two detectives began a quick walk-through of the house. Except for two dead cats in the living room, the front rooms appeared undisturbed, as if an average day had passed in the Coulson home. The front door had been ripped from its hinges by firemen, but no other doors were forced open. An inactivated security alarm system was affixed to the wall near the front door. Rice Krispie treats, uncut in a metal pan, sat on a kitchen counter. A letter rested open on the table. A pocketbook, undisturbed, clearly contained money.

The detectives moved into the front bedroom, but had to go all the way inside, behind a double bed, to see the young girl curled up and lying on the floor. Her hands were tied in front of her body, her feet were bound and three-quarters of her body was blackened by fire. Heading down the hallway, they could see into the bedroom at the end of the house. Another woman, her head distorted by the melted plastic mask and the blaze, was curled up on the floor. She appeared to be pregnant, perhaps halfway through her term. Entering the room, they saw a man lying facedown on the bed. Achetee noticed several packages on the floor beside a dresser and wondered if they were Christmas presents.

"There's two more on the other side of the house," said Bill Lobins, the lead fireman.

Achetee followed him down a short hall, past the washroom and into a narrow hallway lined with shelves crammed with *Popular Mechanics* magazines. The issues dated back decades.

"You'd never know this room was even here,"

Achetee said as he entered a large bedroom that had been carved from two-thirds of a double garage. The remaining garage space served as a woodworking shop. A fireproof wall separated the two rooms.

A smallish man was on the floor, a large woman stretched out on the bed perpendicular to him.

Clearly, the fire had been most intense in this room. The fireproof wall had trapped the flames inside, causing them to lap over the whole room again and again. The woman's body was a charred mass, hands and feet burned off. The man's face was dissolved, yet his clothing remained largely untouched. Ross wrenched the billfold from the man's pants pocket and realized only then that he was Otis Coulson. The family priest, Stuart Hoke, had spoken the wrong names to the bodies as he administered last rites earlier.

Achetee walked outside to interview friends and neighbors while Ross began her crime scene report, measuring, drawing, showing the police photographer what pictures to take. She scoured every inch, looking for the clues she needed to tie a suspect to the murders. The fire made it tough to find evidence. Fire always did.

In a small bedroom converted to a home office, Ross found a tidy stack of papers that indicated Coulson was considering loaning his son Bob $25,000 to buy a windshield repair business. Ross could tell from the numbers neatly printed on a legal pad that Otis Coulson had concluded he could not make the loan. She also found the Coulsons' financial records inside the desk. From stocks, certificates of deposit, and savings accounts, Ross quickly guessed that the Coulsons had accumulated a sizeable estate. She picked up a picture on the desk and looked at it. It showed Mary and Otis

Coulson beaming, surrounded by their children. On the back in a woman's neat hand was written, "25th anny celebration, St. Francis Episcopal Church, Houston, TX, June 20, 1992.

Outside the house, some seventy-five people stood around talking in the hushed tones usually reserved for libraries or museums. A few were crying. Achetee was surprised that everyone seemed to know the family.

"They are . . . er . . . were a very Christian, loving family," neighbor John Hill told him. The others said the same: well-respected, loved. A little girl asked if she could take care of the Coulsons' dachshund, who was inside the fence in the backyard. A policeman got him for her and then freed a box turtle that had been in an aquarium in the kitchen.

By then, most of the people outside knew that five bodies were found in the house.

"Where's Bob?" a man asked.

"Bob?" Achetee asked.

"The Coulsons' son."

"Tell me about him."

The man frowned. "He was a loner, really different from Mary and Otis," the man said. "They were always doing things for people. Otis worked at that co-op that's run by churches, the resale shop, every Friday since he retired. He was a geologist or something. I think at ARCO. Been retired some time, several years. They've lived on this street, gosh, probably fifteen to twenty years. Best neighbors. But Bob. I don't know about him. I just never liked him too much, seemed too . . . I don't know, something."

Achetee found out that a couple of men, transients,

had swept the next-door neighbor's roof about the time of the murders. He jotted down a description.

Another man asked if the murders were tied to Friday the 13th, some sort of Satanic ritual. Achetee wondered if it could have been a drug deal gone bad. As Houston grew and the drug problem worsened, most of the murders in the city were tied to drugs in one way or another, usually drug dealers shooting each other.

"No way," a woman said. "Not this family. They did more work at St. Francis Episcopal than anybody. Mary and Otis both were on the vestry. No, not here."

"That is so far removed from possibility for them," said Bob Tucker, a United Church of Christ minister whose wife, Maggi, was one of Mary's best friends. The Tuckers lived across the street and had a son about Bob's age, Andy. Tucker wondered how he was going to tell his wife about what had happened. Maggi was in Cleveland, due back the next morning when she and Mary were scheduled to go to a handbell convention. Both women were gifted musicians. Mary, a singer, and Maggi, a pianist, spent hours together each week writing religious anthems. Several had already been published. Mary especially was thrilled when the first royalty check had arrived so many years before. She had sent a copy of it to her parents to prove she'd made it as a musician. She was a professional.

At about 8:00 P.M., Chuck Rosenthal arrived at the scene. As is usually the case, the homicide investigators had called for a senior member of the district attorney's office to be present at the crime scene. The burly, silver-haired Rosenthal parked a couple of blocks away and walked briskly toward the Coulson home. He paused momentarily outside the yellow police tape ringing the lot and overheard a man say, "If Bob ain't in there, he did it."

The police issued a statement to the media in time for the *Houston Chronicle*'s early editions. They answered the basic questions, but left alone the one that nagged everyone in Houston: why? Random acts on an untroubled family kindled only one thing: fear. Police said Bob Coulson was out of town and not a suspect. They were looking for him, to tell him that his entire family had been killed.

Sometime after 4 A.M., Detectives Ross and Achetee headed back to the station. Sitting at their desks, they began compiling and sharing information.

"There was such a tremendous amount of violence in that house," Achetee said. "No burglar in his right mind would do that."

"On the cruelty quotient, yeah, it would be cruel," Ross said.

Achetee looked down at his notes. "We really need to find Bob."

Chapter Three

Peter Coulson was grading papers just before 10:00 P.M. on November 13th when the phone rang in his three-bedroom home in San Marcos, 150 miles west of Houston. It was John Hill, a friend of his niece, Robin. Hill had seen the fire, and Peter was the only Coulson relative he knew. Hill, a travel agent, had met Peter when he arranged one of Peter's many vacations.

Even though Hill didn't blurt out the news, the information came at Peter like a rattlesnake on a field mouse.

"There's been a fire at the Coulsons and they've removed five bodies from the house," Hill told Peter, who was seven years younger than Otis. Otis was his oldest brother. Their middle brother Jack lived in California. Peter and Otis were alike in many ways, especially in the painstaking way they approached most things, especially problems. He started dialing phone numbers.

"I have to verify this before I call other family members," he thought. First, Peter called Mary and Otis. Busy. He called the neighbors, the Tuckers. No answer. He called the church. Nothing. Finally, he called the Houston Police Department.

"Sir, I can only verify there has been a fire at the location and there are five casualties," the voice said.

From then until he returned six days later to his snug, little house an easy walk from Texas State University where he taught theater, Peter Coulson operated on autopilot. He knew he had to make funeral arrangements; he was executor of Otis' estate. He would have to call Mary's niece, Linda Payne, who, as of March, was her executrix. Inexplicably, Otis and Mary had changed their wills just eight months before.

They had told their friend and lawyer Jack Emmott they wanted to make changes but they couldn't agree on who should act on their behalf. Rarely, if ever, did the Coulsons argue, especially in front of someone else. But Emmott saw the depth of their disagreement. Otis wanted Peter for his sensibility. Mary wanted Linda for her heart. They agreed to disagree and selected different personal representatives.

Linda Mary Danner Payne was named for the woman everyone in her family called "Auntie Mary." She was their special pal. She had been single for a long time and had often visited, taking the children out to do the fun things their parents could not afford to do with five children.

Linda's husband Tim, a high school assistant principal in Summerville, South Carolina, called her Linda Mary, sometimes just Mary. He knew how much his wife adored her auntie, and he wanted to honor that relationship. He was the only one in the family who used both names. In many ways Tim was Linda's Otis. Balding, stout, Tim Payne looked very much the aging former football player he was. He was ten years older than Linda, who in 1992 was thirty-two. She taught high school students who dreamed of being teachers, and they adored her. As the school disciplinarian, Tim had more than a few kids yearning to be next to drive across his front lawn in the middle of the night. Tim gave Linda the unconditional love she yearned for in her failed first marriage. He was stable, mature, nurturing, all folded into a strong sense of right and wrong.

Peter Coulson thought of Mary's parents, the McEvers, in Knoxville, Tennessee. How could he break the news to them? They had lost their oldest daughter Sarah to breast cancer four years earlier. Remembering that Sarah's husband—and Linda's father—lived in Florence, South Carolina, Peter got the phone number from directory assistance and placed the call. It was close to midnight eastern time.

Peter said he didn't know much, the police didn't know much. All sorts of stories were circulating, gang initiations, drug abusers.

"The one good thing is that Bob was out of town at the time, and wasn't in the house," said Peter. "It's such a strange thing because just last Tuesday Bob came to visit me in San Marcos. He stayed a couple of hours. Everything was terrific."

Coincidentally, all of the Danner family—two sons, three daughters, in-laws, and children—were visiting for an early Thanksgiving. Linda dragged herself from bed before dawn and saw her father sitting in the den, looking grim. He hadn't been to sleep.

"What's wrong?" she asked him. He told her the news.

By 6:00 A.M., all the family was awake, and Bob Danner recounted what he knew. The family sat shocked and silent around the comfortable kitchen.

"Bob did this," Linda's older brother Rick said, finally breaking the silence.

Someone else said, "No one could hate their mother that much."

The Paynes didn't know what to believe. Linda had seen Bob the year before when she went to Houston for Robin and Rick's wedding. In fact, the cousins were paired together often, at the altar, at the reception. She remembered how everyone, especially Mary, commented about how nice looking Bob was in his tuxedo.

"Tell us something we don't know," Robin had said.

About the time the Danner family learned of the murders, Peter Coulson was driving his aged Camry to Houston. The two-hour drive passed like a blur and suddenly Peter found himself sitting in front of Mary and Otis' house. It looked no different than usual, as if the family were inside sleeping gently.

By Saturday morning, thirty Houston police officers worked the Coulson case, chasing dozens of phone tips and scouring the city for the two roofers believed to be on top of the house next door when the Coulsons were murdered. More than a few callers thought it was a cult murder, ritualizing Friday the 13th. Someone reported seeing a suspicious brown van in the neighborhood. The Gulf Coast city of three million was palpably nervous. That morning's *Chronicle* lead the front page with a story headlined "Family found bound, dead in house fire." The report indicated at least one man appeared to have been shot "execution-style in the back of the head" and that other family members were found tied up in their beds. The image seemed too horrible to imagine.

"The violence in this city is just terrible, tragic," a Houstonian told the newspaper. A neighbor of the Coulsons told a television station they feared for their own life because of this unknown, savage killer roaming their previously tranquil street.

Time is a homicide's detective's worst enemy. The more that passes, the less the chance of clearing the case. Dale Achetee and the rest of the Houston Police Department knew that, and they also knew this was a family of some prominence.

"It's an overkill on a drug killing," one policeman said. "And no burglar in his right mind would do this to somebody."

Detective Achetee met the family's lawyer, Jack Emmott, at the house at 10:00 A.M. Stricken with polio as a child, Emmott used a wheelchair to get around. Emmott knew the Coulsons from St. Francis Episcopal church, where he and his wife Dorothy were members. Emmott taught Sunday school and Mary Coulson occasionally was a guest speaker for his class. Mary also was one of the best friends of his mother-in-law Ellen Lansford, also a St. Francis member.

A lawyer in Houston for nearly two decades, Emmott performed legal work on a *pro bono* basis for the church. He had drafted the Coulsons' wills just a few months before. He and Dorothy were at home when the call came from a church member, asking for prayers for the Coulsons. Late that night, the Emmotts went to Jack's office in the Marathon Oil Building to get the Coulsons' file. He thought the church, or possibly police, would need numbers for next of kin or other information.

Saturday morning, Emmott told police he wanted to help them catch whoever did this to his "dear friends." Achetee went inside to get the files; Emmott sat outside.

"They were exactly where I said they'd be," Emmott said later, lauding his friend's scrupulous organizational skills. "Otis would be the kind of person that would keep every piece of paper from the day he was born."

Achetee handed over lists of insurance policies and documents relating to various bank accounts and IRAs. Emmott would need the information when he met with the personal representatives later in the week. First, everyone had to get through the next few days, the visitation, the funeral.

As morning slipped toward afternoon, friends of the Coulsons arrived at the house, drawn by some indistinguishable power to see for themselves that what the papers and television reported was true. Two who came were Mike Scott and Scott Smith, childhood friends of Bob Coulson. The three were in the Spring Woods Senior High School band together, and Bob and Mike had been roommates for a few months earlier that year. Early Saturday, Scott went to Smith's house to pick him up for a golf tournament sponsored by Dannenbaum Engineering, where he worked. Smith numbly showed him the morning paper, and then finished getting dressed. They headed for the golf course, but Mike Scott decided to detour to go by the Coulson home.

"There wasn't any mention of Bob in the article," he told his friend. "I want to know if anybody knew where he was or that he even existed."

Coulson had gone with another friend—and current roommate—Jared Althaus to a cabin in north Texas, Scott told Smith. Jared, a year behind them in school, was working in the same type of drafting job as Scott at Dannenbaum. Scott had heard them at work the day before talking about going to the cabin. They planned to do some fishing. Jared had left early, at about 3:00 P.M.

Mike Scott passed the information on to the police who were standing outside the house.

Inside, Detective Achetee picked up a purse from the kitchen table. Credit cards were still there, he noticed. Then he counted the bills: $163 inside the wallet. Obviously this was no robbery, he thought. The purse was in plain view of anyone who walked into the room.

Achetee walked through the house, pungent with the smell of a soggy campfire. On a desk in what looked like a home office, he noticed a folder with notes written in pencil in a man's precise hand. It was dated August 16, 1992. It seemed to be the remnants of a discussion with Bob Coulson about a business deal. The writer, who Achetee presumed was Otis Coulson, listed assets he would have to liquidate to loan Bob $25,000 to buy a windshield repair business. Otis wrote down his condition: He would only make the loan if Bob would let him look at his financial records. He wanted to see what outstanding bills his son had.

"If you default on the note, then your share of the estate would be equally reduced," Otis wrote.

As the afternoon progressed, Peter Coulson left a series of messages on Bob's answering machine. Where in the world could he be? Peter wondered. He knew his nephew would be devastated when he heard the news and Peter wanted to be there to comfort him.

After lunch in a local cafeteria, Peter met his brother's pastor and the parents of Rick Wentworth at George H. Lewis Funeral Home to make funeral arrangements. It was decided that Robin and Rick would be buried together in Houston, as was the Wentworths desire. The Coulsons would be cremated, as was their wishes, and their ashes sent to Knoxville for burial in Mary's family plot. Her remains would rest beside her older sister's. Peter selected handsome brass containers for the ashes. They set the memorial service for Tuesday morning at St. Francis Episcopal Church.

Peter left the funeral home and drove over to Westview Avenue. He wanted to get the burned mattresses out of the house. He judged them too grisly a sight for Bob. He didn't want his nephew to see the charred places on the bedding where his father, mother and sisters were savagely assaulted.

A man met him there to haul off the matresses. As the one in Mary and Otis' bedroom was removed, Peter found a diary on the box spring. It had been tucked under the mattress. Without looking at it, Peter handed it over to a police detective working in the room.

Chapter Four

The question echoed through the Houston Police Department like a coyote trapped in a mountain canyon. Where's Bob Coulson? Everyone wanted to know. He was the one missing. As they started to compile information about him, police realized he was different from the rest of the family. The others were beloved by friends and neighbors; Bob was described as a loner.

"People really didn't like him," one police investigator reported.

The level of violence in the Coulson home caused police to suspect a family member. Strangers simply don't do that to each other. They don't tie victims' hands, their knees, their ankles. They don't shroud heads with trash compactor bags secured by duct tape and then douse them with gasoline and light a match. This was real anger, deep-seated, sick, stomach-bile fury.

On Saturday morning, police were able to reach Jason

Althaus, the older brother of Bob Coulson's roommate, Jared. Coulson was in a remote cabin near Caldwell in north Texas, Jason said. The two had driven up Friday afternoon. The cabin belonged to Jason's grandfather. They called it "the farm." No phone interrupted the solitude of life there. Television signals barely reached the place. Two hours from Houston, it was perfect for fishing and being alone.

"Tell him his family's been killed and we need to see him," Achetee told Althaus as the young man prepared to drive to the cabin. He liked the idea of helping the police. He was something of a gun enthusiast himself, even loading his own ammunition, and he would have loved to be a policeman.

Althaus had learned of the Coulsons' deaths at about 8:00 A.M. Saturday when Scott Smith had called. He also believed Jared and Bob had gone to the farm. Quickly donning his clothes, Althaus had gone out to get a newspaper and some breakfast for his girlfriend, Deanna. They had read the paper together in horror.

"I need to try to get Jared," he had told her. He had called their apartment and then his parents' house. He couldn't reach anyone. Then the police had called.

Driving singlemindedly along the two-lane roads of the Texas hill country like a rookie on a mission, Jason tried to assemble the right words to tell his brother's friend that his entire family had been savagely slaughtered. He tried to think how the police would handle it on television.

At noon, Althaus pulled onto the dirt road leading to the farm. He got out of the car, looked around at the hushed landscape and told his girlfriend he'd be right back. He walked inside and saw his brother sleeping on a sofa bed and Coulson sleeping on a bed. Awakening, they were startled to see him.

"There's been an accident," Jason blurted out. "Your parents are hurt and you need to go back to Houston to talk to the police."

"What's going on?" Coulson responded, his eyes questioning. "Tell me what happened to them."

"It appears there's been a break-in at their house and the whole family has been killed," Jason said.

Coulson sighed. Jason Althaus searched Coulson's eyes for tears. He didn't see any, but Coulson hung his head and seemed to be sobbing.

"No, God. Oh, no. Oh, my God," he screamed, and ran from the cabin. He went around to the side, where Jason could not see him. Jared walked to the car with his brother.

"Don't let Bob see this," Jason told his brother, as he handed him the morning newspaper. Jason didn't want to upset Coulson any more than he already was. Jared read the paper and then walked over to Coulson. He told him what the paper said, while his brother called police to tell them he had found Bob. They'd be back in two hours.

"Tell them not to stop on the way in," Achetee told him. "Tell them to come straight to the police department."

After Jared packed the car, he and Coulson got inside and followed Jason and Deanna back down the dirt road toward Houston.

It was late afternoon before Bob Coulson showed up at police headquarters in downtown Houston. Red-eyed but wearing pressed clothes that smelled clothes-line fresh, Coulson shook hands firmly with Dale Achetee and followed him into an interrogation room. They sat down in plastic chairs, facing one another.

"Bob, this is going to be very difficult for both of us," Achetee said gently, bending slightly toward Coulson, arms resting on his knees. "I need your complete cooperation and your complete truthfulness. I'm going to ask you questions that are embarrassing. They'll be of a sexual nature, of a financial nature."

"Okay," Coulson said, dabbing at his eyes.

"I need to know what kind of problems your dad was having," Achetee began.

Without hesitating, Coulson said he knew of nothing troubling his father, financial or otherwise. What about Rick or Robin, would anyone hate them enough to do this? Coulson knew of no one. Rick worked as a jailer at the Harris County Jail, but had only been there a few months, not enough time to make enemies. Coulson disclosed that his other sister Sarah had recently had a baby, a boy, who was given up for adoption.

"I don't have any idea how this happened," he said smoothly.

Achetee said, "Well, tell me where you've been since yesterday afternoon."

"We—Jared, my roommate—and I went and got gas," Coulson began. "We had planned this trip for a while. Wanted to go up to Jared's grandpa's for some fishing. It was five when we stopped for gas at the Exxon station near the mall. We drove on up to the farm. We went fishing, went out to lunch, fished some more. Jason came up around one-thirty and told me what had happened."

"Bob, are you queer?" Achetee said abruptly.

"No," Coulson replied without emotion, even though the question seemed to come from nowhere.

"Bob, I'd like to get a statement from you, to put it down on paper," said Achetee. "You're the only one around here who can benefit from it."

Coulson readily agreed, and the two men labored in front of a computer screen for about thirty minutes, looking like colleagues planning a project. They traced the details of Coulson's afternoon. Printed, signed and notarized, the statement was placed on top of a tray on Achetee's desk.

"Bob, I really need your help on this thing," Achetee implored. "I need to eliminate you. Will you take a polygraph? We use it to pinpoint people who didn't do it."

"No, I don't think I could do it," Coulson said, his easy demeanor continuing. "They're really bad and make you look guilty."

Achetee looked Coulson over. He knew no physical evidence tied Coulson to the murders. No fingerprints or shoeprints. No blood. He looked closely for singed hairs on Coulson's arms or face. Nothing. He seemed so calm, cool, talking easily about what he was doing at the same time someone was wrapping a plastic bag around his mother's face. It was as if he were recounting a trip to the grocery store. Achetee thought Coulson unnatural. He wasn't really upset, Achetee thought. Everything seemed too pat. Coulson knew the precise time for everything as if he spent his life with eyes glued to his watch.

Later Achetee would say, "When they know exact

times and shit, they're lying. He didn't say 'I don't know' once.''

Dale Achetee had been through this kind of thing often enough to realize that not every grieving family member flops down on the ground in sheer torment, but Bob Coulson seemed just too detached.

While Achetee was with Coulson, Detective Brad Rudolph took Jared Althaus into another interrogation room. Dark-haired with an olive complexion, Althaus looked nervous. He gave the same account as Coulson. Gas at the Exxon using his credit card, then out to the farm. He handed Rudolph the receipt for the gas, which the policeman copied and gave back. Rudolph closely watched the younger man, trying to see if his body bore any evidence of struggle or being near fire. It didn't. Althaus told him they'd been at the farm since Friday afternoon.

He, too, signed a statement about where he had been when the Coulsons were murdered.

As the two young friends were preparing to leave the station, Achetee asked if he could look inside Coulson's car. It was a black Toyota Celica, a late model, that Achetee discovered actually belonged to Coulson's girlfriend, Jerri Moore, a computer saleswoman whose six-figure income kept Coulson in designer jeans.

Coulson agreed readily to the search. His clothes were neatly folded inside the car. None had burn marks or smelled of smoke. A chest filled with icy wine coolers and beer sat in the backseat. A garbage bag contained a few empties. Nothing.

Achetee told Coulson he'd keep in touch, shook hands and then walked slowly back to his cubicle. He had nothing except a hunch.

"This thing is just not making sense," he told his partner Terry Ross. "I hope we're not getting whipped on it."

There had been another one, back in 1984, that still bothered Achetee. Four members of a family were murdered; the mother and brother as they slept, the father and another brother as they came in the door from work, all shot with the kind of rifle deer hunters use. Prosecutors had tried three times to convict the surviving son of the murders, but failed each time. Whenever the Lewis case came up, Achetee's only comment was: "That little asshole is still walking the streets."

Achetee forlornly told Ross that his gut said Bob Coulson killed his family.

"I'm afraid that bastard is going to walk, too," he said, and Ross knew exactly what he meant.

As soon as Bob Coulson and Jared Althaus finished giving their statements to the police, they drove to the Day's Inn on the Katy Freeway, just off Interstate 10. During the course of the day, Coulson's uncle Peter had left message after message, each one growing more desperate, on the answering machine in his apartment. Peter wanted Bob to contact him just as soon as possible at the motel. He couldn't understand why he couldn't reach Bob.

Just before 10:00 P.M., Coulson and Althaus knocked at Peter's door.

"Bob, I'm glad you're here," Peter said, embracing his nephew.

Coulson introduced his roommate Jared to his uncle. Peter knew Bob had a roommate but had never met him. He seemed like a nice young man, perhaps a little quiet, subdued. Althaus walked over to a small table in front of the television set and sat down. He watched a program and did not speak for the thirty minutes they stayed in the room.

Coulson was hot. Peter had never seen him so agitated before. Coulson said the police were after him. They were hassling him. They accused him of killing his family.

"What?" the older man asked, astonished. Peter tried to reassure his nephew that he would do everything in his power to help him.

"The police insinuated that Jared and I are having a homosexual relationship," he said.

What a ridiculous statement, Peter thought. Coulson had so many girlfriends, such a homosexual relationship seemed ludicrous. The situation had gone from the gruesome to the macabre. It was like a Woody Allen drama, all tragedy, no plot.

"I am angry, too," Peter said. "The police need to be concentrating on who did this and not questioning you."

Coulson was not to be consoled. Finally, he got up to leave and motioned for Althaus to come on. Peter asked if Bob would go to church with him the next morning. He agreed. They made plans to meet outside St. Francis.

Peter's day had been long and he was tired. He changed his clothes and crawled into bed, switching off the light. Peter thought back over the day's events. He felt numb. He couldn't believe the police would suspect Bob of doing such a horrendous thing to his mother and father. As a child, Peter feared losing his family in some sort of freak accident, a car wreck or something. Now, almost the whole Houston Coulson clan was gone. It was as if Houston had dropped off the map or the whole family had moved to Antarctica without leaving a forwarding address.

"There was no one to console," he thought to himself. "Such a total void."

Later Peter would say, "Bob didn't seem to be grieving, but I put it down to macho and that kind of thing."

Chapter Five

Barely thirty-six hours had passed since Stuart Hoke had administered last rites to his beloved parishioners, Mary and Otis Coulson, when he took the pulpit of St. Francis Episcopal Church. He looked out at his stunned flock. Trouble comes with the business of being a pastor, and Hoke was surely used to bolstering ailing, bereaved or dispirited families. This was something else, however. The Coulsons were part of a group that formed the lifeblood of this church, that ten percent who did ninety percent of the work. They rarely said no to a request.

It seemed only right that he fill his sermon with his thoughts on their deaths. Television news crews, hungry to feed on the horrific story, filmed the service. Bob Coulson and his uncle Peter were in the congregation that morning as were a host of the Coulsons' friends.

Hoke, wearing a white robe with a green stole, was a handsome man, thin, with thick brown hair and a moustache. Pushing his glasses toward his forehead, he began his sermon explaining how he had come to be called to the house. He was at the church Friday night, hosting a dinner party for alumni of Episcopal Divinity School, where he earned his degree. Someone called the church and explained the house was on fire and people may have died. He rushed to the scene.

A detective ushered him into the home, which he described as "coming from the nethermost regions of hell—replete with five bodies burned beyond recognition; smoking remains of what had been a warm and wonderful and loving home; intense heat, acrid smell and the tell-tale marks of unmitigated evil under the guise of a horrendous murder."

As Hoke uttered the words "acrid smell," Bob Coulson, sitting two rows from the back, got up and left the large sanctuary. His uncle followed him out. Poor Bob, Peter thought, the description was too much for him. He figured he would stay with his nephew for comfort. Bob's eyes looked red-rimmed, but he did not cry.

Inside, Hoke told the people he felt "shock, pain, sadness, anger and confusion." He admitted his hands and knees started shaking at the Coulson home Friday night and were still shaking that morning. He read from Job, which unknown to him was one oft cited in the journals of Mary Coulson. Job seemed like such a trouper to her. So often she allowed herself to feel trampled upon by her troubles. She called those times her "pity parties."

Hoke cited the morning's Gospel, in which Jesus says, "Not a hair of your head will perish."

"Our Lord's words notwithstanding, not one hair was

to be seen among the remains in this holocaust; the heads of these dear ones were completely charred."

Some in the group wondered why Hoke was so graphic with his description of what he had seen. But this event touched him like no other in his life. He was forever changed. He hurt like never before.

"Of all the families in this world, I can't imagine this family undergoing such horror," Hoke said. "No family should ever have to be so maligned. Especially those who have devoted their lives to the people and things that I preach and you preach are right and good and honorable and godly."

The congregation was shaken to its foundation. Hoke told his members how important it was now for them to realize that dark forces of evil were at work among people who loved God so surely. He hoped the murders would shake up the people, bring them to church and to God in a way they have never been before.

"I cannot believe that these deaths were in vain," Hoke said. "They count for so much more than we shall ever know or sense; with the eyes and ears of faith let us all know that there is meaning and purpose here; that God does bring good out of evil."

Talk about the murders, he implored. Let the grieving begin. Feel the pain. Seek help from friends and family.

"Ask for a hug as many times as you feel you need it," he said.

Many questions arise; few answers exist.

"Say your prayers. Read your Bibles," he said. "It is only through suffering and tribulation and death that life and light and eternity issue in abundance."

As Hoke finished his sermon, Bob Coulson stepped lightly back into the church for communion.

* * *

Szechan Restaurant didn't look like much from the outside, just a small restaurant in a nondescript building beside a commercial street on the outskirts of Houston. But the Chinese food there was unusually good. It was a favorite of Jack Emmott, the family's lawyer. He arranged to meet Bob Coulson and Bob's uncle, Peter Coulson, there for dinner Sunday night. Before day dawned that morning, the younger Coulson called Emmott with questions about his father's estate.

"I understand you're handling the probate of my parents' wills," he said to Emmott, who had been awakened by the phone call. He asked the lawyer how much money was involved.

What a curious question, Emmott thought. His entire family has been savagely murdered and he is wondering about the money?

"Let's get through church this morning and the burial," he told the young man. "We can talk later in the week about these things. Bob, do you think any of Sarah's friends could have done this?"

"No."

"What about Robin's friends?" Emmott wondered, knowing without asking that none of Mary or Otis' many acquaintances could have done such a thing.

"No," Coulson answered.

"You are going through a lot, Bob. You must be worried about your own safety."

"I feel safe," he said.

Emmott noticed that Coulson seemed without emotion, his voice flat, discordant like an untuned piano key. He seemed to ramble, particularly when he told the lawyer about being interrogated by police. Coulson also filled him in on his whereabouts on Friday night and Saturday. Later, at church, Emmott made the dinner plans.

Emmott's wife, Dorothy, a dark-haired, sweet-faced woman who worked with him in his law office, came along for the meal as well.

"The size of the estate is approximately $600,000," Emmott told the men. "Bob, you will either be the sole beneficiary or you will receive half of each parent's estate and Sarah's baby would receive the other half."

Bob Coulson appeared startled.

"What are the child's legal rights?" he asked. He thought the baby had been adopted.

"Bob, I can't act as your lawyer. I represent the estate," Emmott responded.

"I thought the adoption was final," Coulson implored. "I'm surprised he can be an heir."

He asked Emmott for help in finding the baby. That morning, Emmott had told him he did not know where the baby was or which adoption agency had handled the case.

Coulson had also been told that his cousin Linda Payne would represent his mother's estate. He seemed surprised by that as well. Why would she pick his cousin from South Carolina?

During the meal, Bob Coulson laughed at the police and what he considered their bumbling investigation. In the cocky way he had, he berated the investigators and the way they had talked with him the day before. He had spent six hours or so at the downtown headquarters when they should be out looking for the real killer, he said.

The foursome lingered for nearly three hours at the restaurant. When they parted, Emmott didn't like the feeling he had. The next morning, he ordered an alarm system for his home.

Linda and Tim Payne returned to their home in an upscale Summerville, South Carolina, neighborhood Saturday night and prepared to fly to Texas. Otis and Mary's lawyer Jack Emmott called Linda to introduce himself and to talk briefly about the estate.

"You know about the baby . . . ?" he asked.

"Robin's baby?" Linda said.

"No, Sarah's."

"So that was the big secret," she said softly. For months, her Auntie Mary had hinted at some turmoil in their household, but never let on that Mary's twenty-one-year-old, unmarried daughter was pregnant.

Emmott explained that the baby had been put up for adoption but the legal work had not been completed. The baby was an heir.

He also told Linda about the memorial service planned for Tuesday and asked if there was anything he could do for her. He said he'd see her when she arrived in Houston on Monday.

Several times that day, CNN broadcast a report on the murders around the globe. The footage showed workers wheeling gurneys out of the smoldering house, almost tipping one of them over when it hit the side of the curb. It looked like a large body underneath the body bag. It could have been her Auntie Mary.

Linda went upstairs to a room she used as an office. She and Tim lived in the four-bedroom house in which

Tim had reared his two, now grown, children from a previous marriage. It was much too big for them, but Linda had jumped in contently and refurbished every room. They had not yet been married a year.

Usually gregarious, Linda felt like someone had beaten her up. Her body ached. She sat down at her desk and glanced at the wall. A cross-stitch picture that Mary made for her hung there. It said, "Every season has its gift for living."

Linda got out her copy of the will and read it and the letter Mary had sent with it. "Don't panic," Mary had written. "I figure I've got another fifty years at least." It was dated April 28th, seven months earlier.

Linda made reservations to fly to Houston and sat up most of the night. She felt heartache like she had never before. Sunday filled up with packing and telling friends and coworkers the news. Linda drew up lesson plans for the person who would teach her classes.

Sunday night, the Paynes lumbered into their Charleston-style rice bed, which was a good foot higher than a conventional bed, and snuggled. Linda cried anew as she lay in her husband's arms, feeling some semblance of warmth and normalcy. The phone rang and Linda reached to answer.

"Linda?" the man's voice said, cold and clipped. It was Bob Coulson. Linda jumped to her feet. His voice was like steel. She knew who it was even before he told her.

"I had dinner tonight with Jack, Dorothy and Peter and found out you're involved in the will."

"Yes, I'm executrix," she said.

"When did she do that?" he asked, referring to his mother changing her personal representative.

"Bob, I'm really sorry this has happened," Linda said, her voice sympathetic. "I can't believe this has happened to you."

"We were at the cabin," he said abruptly. "Now the police are harassing me. I want them to leave me alone so I can get on with my life."

Linda told her cousin how much it meant to their grandparents to have his parents and sister buried in Knoxville.

"Yeah, I had planned to have them all buried there but the Wentworths want Robin here. Rick wasn't a member of our family."

"I know you'll want to come to Knoxville," Linda said. "You need to let them know when you can come."

"Well, whatever," he said. "I need to know when your plane is getting in. I'll pick you up." Linda tried to convince him there was no need; they were renting a car. She was having trouble thinking clearly; she was literally freaked out by Bob's demeanor. She told him that Tim had made the reservations and she didn't have the details. She would see Bob the next day. Linda could only wonder: could Bob have done this?

After an uneventful flight, Linda and Tim stepped off the plane and made their way up the jetway. They saw a solitary figure standing at the airport entrance, a silhouette framed in light. He looked like the Marlboro man. It was Bob.

He gave Linda a stiff hug and said, "Look at my eyes." He dug his fingernails into the purplish lower lid. Linda saw him do that often over the next few days. No real tears flowed from this boy, Linda thought.

Coulson showed them to his girlfriend's Toyota. Settling into the car, Coulson said, "I can't believe the stupidity of the Houston police. They are harassing me. I may have to sue them for harassment. They fingerprinted me and even took a side of my handprint. I wish they'd get on the right track and look at how hard this is on me. Look at my eyes."

Linda said softly, "I know you've been through a lot."

Coulson explained again he had been fishing at a remote cabin.

"If you drive like my father it takes three and a half hours to get there," he said. "If you drive like a normal person it takes two and a half."

Linda noticed the inside of the car was immaculate. No clutter. The only item in the car was a tube of toothpaste and a toothbrush in a side pocket.

"Well, now I find out that this stuff about the baby may not be right," Coulson interjected. "You didn't know about the baby?"

"No, none of us knew, not even Granny and Dicko," Linda said, referring to her mother's parents.

"My mother underestimated everybody, especially me," Coulson said. "She called everybody together to tell about Sarah's baby. Ugh! Robin had to always be in control. She was such a bitch about everything. Now my dad's lawyer is telling me that the adoption was not final. The baby gets half the money."

Coulson dropped them at the luxurious Doubletree Hotel on Houston's pricey Post Oak Boulevard. He said he'd see them later at the funeral home. Once he was gone, Linda turned to her husband and said, horror-stricken, "Oh, Tim, he did it!"

Chapter Six

Bob Coulson and the few remaining relatives gathered at the George Lewis Funeral Home Monday night to receive friends. Such an event is distinctively Southern, a rite that brings out the best and worst in people. It's not unusual for total strangers to be in a receiving line and to say, "I knew her!" when they gawk into an open casket. Of course, for the Coulsons there would be no open casket. In fact there were only two caskets, a situation that puzzled many people.

"Who is in there?" Linda Payne heard people ask. Most people didn't know that Otis, Mary and Sarah had been cremated. Linda felt awkward. She knew only a handful of people. Some folks looked sad, others scared.

Bob Coulson stood on one side of the caskets, the Wentworths on the other. Nodding his head, offering a stiff hug, he seemed the grieving son. He looked like the star of the show.

Linda wanted desperately to leave. It must have showed on her face. Dorothy Emmott, the wife of the family lawyer, told her she ought to go back to the hotel. It didn't take much convincing.

"This is misery," she told her husband, Tim.

Linda walked over to Coulson and told him she was leaving.

"No, stay," he said. "I'll take you back to the hotel."

She told him that wasn't necessary; they were leaving.

"Is there anything I can do before I go?" Linda asked.

He leaned over and in a conspiratorial tone and said, "Yeah, take my place in line and talk to these old people."

When Coulson saw Ken Smith, the father of his good friend Scott, he pulled him out of the line and into a small waiting room. Smith looked into Coulson's red eyes, noticing the eyes seemed puffy and the eyelids were red. He didn't see any tears but he assumed Coulson's eyes were red from crying.

"What have you heard?" Coulson asked the older man. "What's on the news?"

Smith told him what he had seen.

Coulson also wanted to know if the police had contacted Ken. The police were putting a lot of pressure on him, he said.

"They're all over me."

Sunday afternoon, Detective John Swaim visited Jared Althaus at the apartment he shared with Bob Coulson. It was a nice complex, the kind of place where young working people lived when they were just starting out. Tall, thin, clean-cut, Jared Althaus looked like a man who had never known trouble. He and Coulson had met in high school, but only recently decided to room together.

Jason Althaus, Jared's older brother, had told Swaim earlier that Jared seemed distraught, perhaps overly so. Jason had confided that Jared wasn't eating or sleeping. He seemed tied up in knots.

"He's got the shits bad," Jason had said.

When pressed, a seemingly confident Althaus backed up Coulson's story word for word. Gas, cabin, fishing, lunch. That's what they did. He even produced the credit card receipt for the gas, stamped with the time: 5:06 P.M. No way was he anywhere near the house on Westview. The gas station was a good fifteen miles north of the Coulson home, heading out of town.

Swain thanked him politely for his time and started out the door.

"One more thing, Jared," he said, "will you take a lie detector test?"

"I had to take one of those things before," Althaus said, twisting his hands together. "It said I was lying and I wasn't. It cost me my job. I ain't taking it."

Swaim left even more convinced that Althaus held the key to solving the riddle. He planned to step up the pressure. Monday afternoon, he visited Althaus at his workplace, Dannenbaum Engineering. His boss said Bob Coulson had come in some time before noon and shortly afterward Althaus had asked for the rest of the day off.

"Jared was really upset," the boss said.

Althaus had left the building, gone home, packed a bag and headed out of town. He went to San Marcos to see his girlfriend, a student at Southwest Texas College. San Marcos police tracked Althaus' car to the parking lot of a small motel, where they sat watching it for more than an hour while Houston detectives drove over in a Dodge minivan.

A loud rapping on the motel's hollow door resounded across the quiet parking lot. Swaim and the other police officers heard shuffling and mumbling and what sounded like a chair being knocked over. Althaus, disheveled and partially dressed, meekly opened the door. It seemed obvious that the detectives had disturbed him and his girlfriend.

Althaus went out to the van to talk to the officers. They went over and over the story. Gas, cabin, no knowledge of anything until Jason found them Saturday. He hadn't seen the Coulsons in months. He had not been in their house on Friday. He knew nothing.

After two hours, Swaim looked at Althaus and said, "Good enough. But I want to leave you with one thought, Jared. You ain't never going to be able to live with this and Bob is not going to let you live with it. He's going to have to kill you."

Althaus did not respond.

En route back to Houston, Swaim called Achetee. "I don't think this kid has anything to do with it," Swaim said, changing his mind.

Achetee was crestfallen. Without Althaus, they had nothing. Achetee told Ross to go home; nothing more could be accomplished. In the morning, they would start back on the phone tips: the strange brown van in the neighborhood, cult figures, devil worshippers, odd characters who seemed to slither from the darkness whenever baffling murders occurred.

Achetee looked at the *Chronicle*. Page One again. The

city surged with fear. The Coulsons' neighbors said they couldn't sleep. They jumped at every noise from outside. They left floodlights on and installed security alarms. No one seemed to notice that the Coulsons had done the same within six months of their deaths.

As the detectives raced toward San Marcos to find Jared Althaus, Bob Coulson was basking in the glow of his friends' sympathy. About a dozen of his friends from high school gathered at the home of Jessica Guidry. A bunch of them had planned to go on a trip together but postponed it to attend the wake at the funeral home. There, they told Coulson to meet them afterwards at Jessica's house.

He walked in, and talked with his friends. Everybody wondered where Althaus was. No one had seen him. They thought it odd that he didn't come to the visitation. Coulson told them Jared was out of town. He had left early from work, in fact.

Coulson looked tired, several friends said, and they noticed how red his eyes were. They just couldn't believe such a thing had happened to their friend. He didn't really want to talk about it. He seemed so quiet, so hurt.

Coulson huddled in the corner with Mike Scott, his friend from high school, and asked what was being printed in the press about the murders. He also wanted to know what the police were asking his friends.

Scott had talked with the police once briefly at the house Saturday. The papers had stories every day, including pictures of the family. One picture used often came from the church directory. That morning, sketches of two possible witnesses, the roofers, ran on the front page. A friend was quoted as saying the family "wouldn't hurt a fly." He said they were the last people in the world he would expect to be murdered.

"I've decided which cars to keep," Coulson told his friend. He was trying to decide what to do with the lot the house sat on. He thought it might be nice as a park, to memorialize his family. It might be tough to sell the house with its history.

"I think I can get about half a million in cash pretty quick," he proudly told the friend.

From across the room, a woman said to her friend, "He must not want to talk about it." The women looked over at Coulson. He had such a way about him. Women just naturally noticed him and enjoyed being with him.

A friend remembered later how glad everyone was that Coulson had come over.

"We all just wanted to spend some time with him," she said.

Coulson stayed about 45 minutes before going home.

Close to midnight, Detective Dale Achetee decided to go home. A bachelor, he didn't have anyone to go home to, but the long days were taking a toll. Walking down a hallway, he almost ran into Jared Althaus.

"I drove one hundred miles per hour to get back here," Althaus said to Achetee, who he had met briefly the night Coulson was questioned.

Achetee was almost in tears. He knew Althaus was ready to burst.

"Come on in the back, son," Achetee said, smiling slightly as he realized that Althaus must have passed Detective Swaim on the highway.

"I was never inside that house," Althaus said quickly as they sat down.

Like many people who have committed horrible crimes, Althaus seemed quiet and unruffled as he finally let out the secret he had held for three days. He wore light-colored blue jean shorts and a tee-shirt.

"We've been planning this for four months," he began. "Bob just mentioned it one day and I don't know, it just seemed intriguing. He mentioned it like jokingly or I thought it was jokingly and then it became conversation and he got like, 'Gee it would be nice not to ever have to work again, all that money,' just kept talking about it. He told me we'd live in a nice place and have everything we ever wanted. He didn't want to have to work again.

"He didn't ever say he hated his parents. He just said he probably wouldn't ever miss them. We kept talking about it and thought of ways to do it. He didn't want a way that he would have to actually kill them himself. That's when he thought of the bags over their heads."

"What do you mean, Jared?" Achetee asked, dumbfounded that the young men could separate their actions from what happened to the family.

"He said it wouldn't be like killing them, they would suffocate. But he thought he should have some type of gun, just in case. We went to a gun shop together and bought a stun gun. It was a place on Highway 6 in a strip shopping center."

"What other tools did you get?"

"One day I was looking for a headboard and dresser and we stopped in a store and got zip cords, three for each of the five people, tape. That was about three months ago. Another day Bob told me he got trash bags, trash compactor bags, because he thought they wouldn't rip as easily.

"Last Thursday we bought a gasoline can and filled it up. We took it over to his parents and asked if we could store it in their garage. He told them it was mine and my dad was cleaning out our garage and we needed a place to keep it.

"Bob was trying to figure out a way to cover it up so he decided to burn the whole house down. He was going to pour gas over everything and then maybe get some Varsol from the garage. I was to drop him off about a block away, drive over to 290 and get gas and drive around. Then go back and pick him up.

"I dropped him off around four-fifteen and was supposed to pick him up at six. He wasn't there so I made a circle, circled again and the third time around he was there. He was wearing a dark blue sweatshirt he had turned inside out, dark jeans, a baseball cap, sunglasses and tennis shoes, high tops.

"He had already put the supplies in the house that Thursday afternoon when no one was home. He took my medium gray Eastpak and put the zip cords, the stun gun, tape, matches inside and hid it in the attic.

"We picked that day because it was the weekend and we could get out of town. We didn't have anything to do and it was after the time change so it would be darker. He told his family he wanted to meet to tell them about some big plans he had for a business. He told his mother he'd be there at four-fifteen, and he told Robin and Rick to be there at five-fifteen.

"He got back in the car, smelling like gas, and said, 'It went all wrong.' We drove around and threw all the stuff out of the car into ditches along the road. He told me he got his mother into the garage bedroom by telling her he wanted to show her his dad's Christmas present. He stunned her with the stun gun and it didn't work. He told her he needed money and they wouldn't get hurt. They struggled and he tied her up on the bed and got a pillow and tried to smother her. He got her tied up and put the bag over her head. Then he got his father and took him back to the bedroom and did the same thing. He said his father was no trouble.

"Then he went into Sarah's room. She looked up at him and said, 'I love you,' and he said, 'I love you too, babe.' He put the plastic bag over her head and she didn't struggle.

"He was in the bedroom with Sarah when Robin and Rick came into the house. It startled him but he got them back to his parents' bedroom. He told them to get down and not to move. He told them I was in the other room with a gun on mom and dad. He ran out into the garage and got a crowbar and hit Rick with it and then hit Robin with it. He started putting gas on and the hot water heater set it on fire. He poured gas on everybody. He hurried, grabbed all his stuff and got out of the house.

"He showed no remorse. No regrets. It was just for the money."

Tuesday morning dawned with a cloudless fall sky, the kind of Texas day that helps make up for all the hot, humid days of summer. But the friends and the little family that survived Mary and Otis Coulson hardly noticed. It was the day to say goodbye to a family that police were discovering was close to fairy-tale perfect.

They never managed to dig up any dirt on Mary and Otis Coulson.

Wearing a gold-braided, off-white vestment, The Reverend Stuart Hoke looked out over the pulpit to the brick and wooden sanctuary of St. Francis Episcopal Church to see every pew filled. Bob Coulson, dressed in a somber gray suit, sat in the front row with his uncle Peter Coulson and Rick Wentworth's parents, Wayne and Elise. Linda and Tim Payne chose the third row back. She wanted to be unobtrusive, plus she wanted to be able to watch Bob. They had met moments earlier in the small room behind the sanctuary, the same room where the family gathered before Robin's wedding two years before. When Coulson saw Linda just before the funeral, he stretched out his arms and pulled her close. "Love you guys," he said, rigidly.

As the service began, Peter placed his arm around his nephew and rubbed his back. Coulson looked down at the floor. Every now and then he would hold his head back as if he were looking up at the sky. St. Francis had been like a second home to him as he was growing up. He was an acolyte, the Episcopal version of an altar boy.

Many in the congregation cast shy glances toward Coulson, empathizing with him in the bottomless sorrow of a family lost. They willingly accepted the police statement that Coulson was not a suspect. He may be somewhat aloof and cocky, but he was no murderer in the eyes of the people who watched him grow to adulthood. Some had called the Houston police chief to complain about Coulson being harassed by detectives. Peter Coulson was one.

"It's time to look for the real murderers," he told a detective who had called him for information.

Linda looked around the sanctuary and was struck by the mix of people. Upper middle-class couples sat beside long-haired hippie types. Good old boys, working men. Linda suspected every walk of life was represented in the church this day. What a testimonial to the lives of her Auntie Mary and Uncle O.

Hoke was jittery. He had been sickened, stunned, horrified by the scene he had seen three days earlier at the Coulsons' home. Hoke had been at a dinner at the church and picked up the phone absently.

"There's a fire at the Coulson house," the man had told him. "You're needed immediately. Everyone in here is dead."

In twenty years as a priest, he had never been called to the scene of a murder and had never had to find the right words to comfort a panicked congregation. Every one of the 600 members of the upscale church knew or knew of Mary and Otis Coulson. They both served on the governing board and sang in the choir. Occasionally, Mary had performed a solo and had been asked by many a St. Francis bride to sing *The Lord's Prayer* at her wedding. Mary also had taught the University of Sewanee extension program that provided theological education for lay people.

Thinking back over all her friend had meant to St. Francis, Ellen Lansford remembered a talk on the prayer book Mary gave last year. "People are still saying how it helped them look at the prayer book in a whole new way," she thought.

Later Ellen described her friend Mary by saying, "People look out of different windows and sometimes they can explain what they see. Mary saw things the rest of us didn't see."

" 'I am the resurrection and the life,' saith the Lord," Hoke intoned as the service began. He had written a sermon about faith, challenging the people to hold fast even as they faced a time they did not understand and could barely comprehend.

He told of a letter Mary had written the previous month to a friend whose mother had just died. "I wanted to share a thought with you that I hope will bring comfort as you move through your grief," Mary wrote. "Those who love God never see each other for the last time."

"So dear, Mary," the priest said. "may your soul and that of Otis and Robin and Richard and Sarah, and the souls of all the faithful departed though the mercy of God, rest in peace."

Linda wept silently, Bob Coulson looked up at the ceiling. Detective Achetee, standing in the back, watched solemnly. Policemen watched from every corner. The service continued on the side of a hill at a cemetery far from town, where Robin and Rick were buried. The police had stopped traffic on all six lanes of Interstate 20 the entire length of their trip to the cemetery.

Church members provided lunch after the graveside ceremony. In the South, usually a meal is brought to the family home for survivors. In this case, there were few survivors and no family home. They gathered in the fellowship hall at about noon. In that way people have when they simply don't know what to say, few people spoke of the Coulsons. Linda was picking at her food when one of the assistant ministers walked up and said heartily, "Heaven is a much louder place now that Mary is there."

Linda laughed out loud. It felt good to have someone speaking of her Auntie. And that surely was a true statement.

Bob Coulson walked over to her.

Linda said, "Where is that roommate of yours? I just want to hug his neck for being so good to you."

Coulson looked away and said curtly, "I just don't know. Nobody has seen him. I'm sure he went out of town to visit friends. I'm sure there is a message at the apartment. I'm going there now."

After the meal, Coulson walked his girlfriend, Jerri Moore, to her car and parked about a block from the church. They hugged and kissed goodbye and he turned to walk back to the church. He did a little kick step as he strolled along the street, but then righted his posture immediately when he saw someone coming out of the church.

Jared Althaus told three different stories before he told the one he swore to police was the truth. They had him give another statement to the Houston Fire Department Arson Division and meet with Arson Investigator Buddy Woods. Then they put his story to the test.

Detective Brad Rudolph brought Althaus back to the police department, gathered some gear and headed out with the suspect and two other officers. It was about 10 o'clock in the morning, the Coulsons' memorial service had just begun. Jared showed them the way of the crime, beginning at the Coulsons' house. They retrieved a number of the items Althaus said Coulson had thrown out of the window of Jerri's car four nights earlier. The crowbar was hanging in a tree limb in a ditch. The red plastic gas can was in another ditch.

After stopping for fries and shakes, they found the blue sweatshirt Althaus said Coulson wore to murder his family, a blue baseball cap, the gray backpack and the ski mask. The items were strung all along the 150 miles between Houston and Caldwell, where the farm is located.

They called in a dive team to search a small creek for the gun Coulson held on Robin and Rick. It was found several days later, in pieces. Althaus dozed for a time in the car.

Police on horseback searched portions of the road, looking for the pants and the shoes Coulson wore. Althaus said Coulson's pants and shoes were bloodied when he struck Rick in the head with the crowbar. Blood splattered all the way across the room and onto the window. Investigators never found the pants or shoes, a blow to the case, but not a fatal one, the prosecution believed.

Lab tests revealed no fingerprints on any of the items found, but police could tie them to Coulson with Althaus' testimony. And now they had him on their side. Somehow, he had broken the hold Bob Coulson had on him.

Chapter Seven

The police informed Peter Coulson and Linda Payne that the investigation at the house would be completed Monday, so it would be wise to get the valuables out because it would be unattended. They agreed to meet there the afternoon after the memorial service.

Linda was the first to arrive. The front door was kicked in, but she was surprised at how normal everything looked. She opened the door and felt like she had entered hell. The power was still off, leaving the house dark in the midday drizzle. A wet smoke smell permeated everything. Black was the primary color. Linda walked from room to room. The curio cabinet was black, but most everything looked as Mary had left it. The coffeepot was half-full. Her knitting was sitting out and a library book was open on a table. Linda headed toward her aunt's bedroom to retrieve her jewelry. She saw two large maroon-colored shopping bags from Foley's Department Store beside the bed.

"Christmas presents," she thought. "That is so like Auntie Mary to be shopping for Christmas presents in November."

Linda peeked inside. She tried to figure out who the gifts had been bought for: nine Christmas ornaments—grandniece and grandnephews; heart-shaped pin cushions—nieces; flannel shirts—brother-in-law.

When Mary had asked Linda to be her executrix, Linda had wondered why her Auntie had picked her. Besides being her namesake, Linda Mary carried on the most correspondence with her aunt over the years. But Linda was the fourth of Mary's sister's five children and was just thirty-two years old.

"Are you sure you want to do this?" Mary had asked. Now, the words came back to Linda. It seemed odd to be asked twice when you've made an important decision. Had Mary been afraid of something?

Peter Coulson retrieved a number of sentimental items, including his brother's clarinet. He also found a 35-millimeter camera and a camcorder, some coins and a horde of priceless family pictures.

Linda looked around her Auntie's room, which had been redecorated only three months earlier. White paint flaked from the closet door; the fancy flowered shower curtain she was so proud of had melted. Perhaps twenty of Otis' ties had turned into curls of black string. A case of Clinique makeup was melted to the dresser. Absently, Linda looked down and saw a charred spot where Robin's body had been. She methodically began sorting through the jewelry, picking out the real from the fake, the sentimental from the worthless. The large

silver cross that Mary so often wore lay in the box. Linda
tucked it inside her pocket.

Voices drifted in from the front of the house, making
their way toward her. Bob Coulson stood in the doorway,
grinning from ear to ear. He wore light blue and white-
striped shorts, a tank top and tennis shoes.

"You can see there was a body right here," he said,
shining a flashlight on the carpet.

Linda turned around and saw three neighbors behind
Coulson. They were about his age. One looked embarrassed.

"We just saw Bob here and we stopped to tell him
we're sorry . . ." his voice trailed off.

"Wait till you see this," Coulson told them as he
guided them to Sarah's bedroom. The young men
moved out and eventually left the house.

"Hello, hello," Coulson said in a voice that sounded
like Elmer Fudd. "Where are you? What are you all
doing?"

Coulson asked Tim if he'd help cover the hole in the
roof the firemen had cut for ventilation. Tim said he'd
hold the ladder while Coulson climbed up top. Before
Coulson set the plywood in place, he looked through
the hole in the roof just as Linda, standing in the room
below, looked up at him. She said later his face emitted
evil as it was framed by the roof. Coulson completed his
task and jumped down from the roof. Linda wondered
about his knee that supposedly was so damaged he could
not work.

Coulson asked if Linda had found any journals. She
hadn't.

Linda told her husband, "I have got to get out of
here."

They moved toward the car, but Coulson stopped them.

"Linda, your hands are terrible. Wash your hands," he said, leading her toward an outside spigot hidden behind a six-foot-tall evergreen bush on the neighbor's house. It provided a perfect perch to watch everything that went on in the Coulsons' house.

"Shhh!" he said. "It's a secret place."

Linda could only wonder whether Coulson had hidden there before.

They all drove to the home of church friends, who graciously invited Peter Coulson to stay with them. Sitting in a circle in a bedroom, Peter said they should divide the items up for safekeeping. He picked up three plastic bags with names written in marker on the outside. It was the personal effects that were on the bodies and removed when the autopsies were done. He handed Coulson the bag containing Otis' watch, wedding band and the $89 he had had in his billfold.

"No, no. I don't want any of it," Coulson said, refusing to hold his hand out to accept the bag.

Peter handed him the cash, but Coulson raised his hand and said, "No, I really don't want it or need it. You keep it."

"Everybody can use money," said Peter. Everyone in the room encouraged Coulson to take the money and finally he gave in.

Linda handed Mary's bag to Bob, saying, "There's some very nice rings in here; you'll want them later."

"I don't want it," he replied. Linda put the bag aside. She would keep it safe.

Linda showed him Sarah's jewelry and for the first time, Coulson seemed interested. He pulled a necklace from the plastic bag and held it in the palm of his hand. "I'll keep this," he responded. "I'm sure some of Sarah's friends would want it."

Linda wondered why he showed such interest in Sarah's things but none for anyone else's. Just what was their relationship, she thought.

Peter offered Coulson some old pictures of his parents, but he rejected them.

"I always hated those pictures," he replied.

Then Peter pulled out some old coins. Coulson started showing some interest in those. He also decided to keep the camcorder, cameras and the VCR.

Walking out to the car, Coulson turned to Tim and said, "I've never seen a camcorder worth less than six hundred dollars, have you?"

Chapter Eight

The final part of Jared Althaus' agreement with police was the one that turned him inside out. Althaus had already been nauseous for days, ever since he had dropped Coulson off at his parents' house on Friday. But the final hurdle would be crossed when he confronted Coulson Tuesday night at the Motel 6 on Interstate 10. Police wanted him to entice Coulson into confessing.

A microphone hidden in the room picked up and recorded their conversation. Police technicians listened from the room next door.

Shortly before 9:00 P.M., half a day since his parents' memorial service, Coulson rapped on the metal door. Althaus answered and said abruptly, "I'm scared as shit. They fucking came up there to talk to me."

Coulson looked at his overwrought roommate and said, "Okay, let me do the talking okay? Just answer yes or no, okay? You went up to see Rebecca?"

"Yes."

"And you told her that you wanted to go see her."

"Yeah."

"Look at me. Let me explain something to you now."

Coulson's voice was steady, patient, like a doctor explaining an ear infection to a small child.

"They went into my parents' house and took every file that my dad had, okay, files and files because they're trying to find out why somebody would do this. Okay?"

"I didn't kill your fucking parents, Bob," Althaus pleaded.

"Uhm," Coulson said.

"I don't want to go to jail, Bob."

"Hey, look at me, Jared. If they had something okay I want an understanding here, okay. Now if they come to question you again, tell them that you want to have a lawyer present."

"I don't need a lawyer, Bob. I didn't go . . ."

"What did they say?"

"They told me that somebody saw a black car pulling out. They can identify the car being there."

"Jared, if somebody saw a car, maybe they saw a car. Okay? They have to prove beyond a reasonable doubt that it was us. They have to prove, they have to disprove our alibi. I'm your alibi. You're my alibi. We told them what happened. You've got to be strong, okay?"

"I don't want to go to jail," Althaus said.

"Are you hearing me?" Coulson responded. "Are you hearing what I'm saying? You're not listening. They have to prove beyond a reasonable doubt who was in the fucking car, what fucking car it was. Do you know how many black Celicas there are in the city of Houston?"

"Yes, I know Bob."

"Hey, I need you to be strong for me, man. Whatever you do, don't panic. Okay? What I'm telling you is not bullshit. This is what's going on. My uncle had to go back in there with them to get all of the shit out. If you were a police officer and you had a lead, y'all were going to nail somebody, would you fucking do that shit?"

"No," Althaus answered.

"No, it's wasted man-hours."

"I did tell them, Bob."

"One more thing, the phone is our enemy, we need to be careful about the phone, okay?"

"I'm sorry, Bob."

"Hey, hey, man, hey. I love you, man, I'm sorry. But let's get through this. Okay? I'm serious. I'll be there for you and you be there for me, okay?"

"Okay."

Althaus whimpered like a lost kitten, pleading with Coulson to make things right. The two went on for twenty minutes or more as Coulson tried to calm his fears. Althaus told Coulson the police were pushing him to take a polygraph test. Coulson said he'd hire a lawyer to keep Althaus safe. Coulson said he would agree to a test provided police would leave Jared alone.

"Don't say anything," he said. "Okay, Jared? Hey be there for me man, okay? Be there for me."

"I knew it wasn't going to be easy."

"Don't cry," Coulson said, holding his friend's hand. "Don't quit now. You gotta be strong, man, okay?" He continued softly, "Even if it went to court, we just swear that that is what happened. They have got to prove beyond a reasonable doubt and there's not a jury in the fucking world that will convict the two of us after we get a hundred fucking people up there saying we're great. They can't find somebody that can identify us. They haven't even touched me. They haven't questioned me. They must have picked up when we were being questioned that I was solid and I wasn't, you know, going to break down. You know what you have to do."

"Stick to the alibi?"

"Yes."

"What if someone saw something? Throw something out or something?"

"Let me tell you something. They didn't see nothing, okay. Be strong for a little bit longer, please, okay. At least look and go to work and act like everything's fine, and see what happens, if nothing happens who's fucking right? Tell me. You're fucking with me, man. I will never change the story, you will never change the fucking story."

Coulson asked Althaus to go have a margarita with him, but Althaus said he just wanted to stay in the motel. Coulson wanted him to go home. Althaus said he would leave as soon as he saw Coulson pull out of the parking lot.

"You there for me?" Coulson asked.

"Yeah."

"I'm there for you."

"Uh huh."

"My boy?"

"Yeah."

"You okay?"

"Just go ahead. I'll just go in there and I'll open and shut the door. I'll leave in five minutes."

As Bob Coulson stepped outside the room, police officers surrounded him and placed him under arrest.

Inside the police van, Coulson told the officers he wanted to cooperate but some questions would be too emotional.

"Can I just talk about what happened?" Coulson asked. "Well, I guess you think I hated them. I did not hate them. I got myself in such a financial bind, this was the only way out."

Detective John Swaim asked Coulson, "Did you intend for the entire family to be there?"

Coulson paused for a long time before he replied, "That's one of those questions that's too emotional."

The van phone rang and the assistant district attorney on the case, Chuck Rosenthal, told the officer to take Coulson before a magistrate to have his rights read to him. No screwups with this one, he said. Swaim and the other detectives just shook their heads. Coulson had started talking, but now would stop. Anybody who talked after having their rights read by a judge was an idiot. Coulson was a lot of things, but he wasn't an idiot.

Cameramen swarmed the police station as Bob Coulson was led inside after his arrest. Wearing a white tank top and navy blue shorts, he was escorted down the wide halls toward the booking office. He entered the elevator, turned around to face the front and stared straight into the hot lights and the television cameras. A slender smirk remained planted on his face.

A day after Coulson's arrest, he called Ken Smith, the father of his childhood friend Scott Smith. Coulson seemed confused, upset, maybe even preoccupied. Two days later, Ken and Jerri Moore visited Coulson in jail. He was ushered into a small Plexiglas cubicle, with a small grill through which to talk. Wearing a jailhouse orange jumpsuit, Coulson sat down. He looked subdued, defeated, even embarrassed, Smith noticed.

"Did you kill your family?" Smith asked, almost immediately.

"Ken. It came up and it wouldn't go away," Coulson responded.

"Why?"

"Everything was falling apart. Money wouldn't get better. Everything was coming to pieces. It kept coming up and we did it."

Smith couldn't believe what he was hearing. He'd known this young man for years. His son Scott and Bob were childhood pals. They had worked on cars, side by side, many times.

He stepped away from the cubicle to give Jerri the opportunity to speak with Coulson.

"No matter what happens, I'll always love you," Coulson said to her when she sat before the Plexiglas window.

Jerri, with words, attacked Coulson like a viper.

"Do you have AIDS," she demanded.

He was stunned. Where the fuck did this come from? He was expecting his friends to come to see him and be understanding and sympathetic. Instead, they accused him. They thought he did it. He hadn't slept since he'd been in jail. People kept bugging him and hassling him. Now he had these two on him.

Jerri felt confused and angry. She was shocked. Here is this man she had been intimate with, who she even thought she could have married, charged with killing his family in the most brutal of ways.

"I don't have AIDS," he said.

"Have you taken any money from me?" she charged back.

"No."

"Have you been dating other women?"

"Yes," he responded.

"In my car?" She couldn't believe this.

"No."

Jerri wanted to know if he slept with other women at her house. He said he had not.

Finally, she said, "Did you kill Sarah first?"

He put his head down and answered, "My, God, no."

He then said, "All Jared did was pick me up and drop me off."

Coulson looked at her and said, "If we had gone to lunch, this wouldn't have happened."

"My God, Bob, you're telling me if I had gone to lunch with you, five people would be alive today?"

Jerri remembered talking with Coulson shortly after the murders and he speculated about the killings. He said his father would have been easy to put down; his mother probably fought the hardest. And she remembered him calling her to warn her to stop talking to Jared. It was upsetting Jared, all the questions about what happened. Her feelings all along seemed so right. Bob had done it.

Smith went back to see Coulson in December. This time Coulson seemed more lucid. He told Smith he did not kill his parents. Smith had misunderstood him, he said.

PART II:
The Family

Chapter Nine

For a woman who vividly remembered wondering whether she would ever marry, Mary Coulson felt decidedly melancholy as she and her husband Otis drove into the parking lot of St. Francis Episcopal Church for their twenty-fifth wedding anniversary celebration. It was June, hot, sticky, Texas-style summer, 1992. It would be a small gathering, just the closest of their many friends and acquaintances. They had agreed; they didn't care to fling out their heartache like a soiled tablecloth at a family reunion for people they barely knew.

Otis pulled Mary's white Camry into a space near the side door, shut off the engine and looked at his wife. She had gained sixty pounds, maybe more, since they married, but to him, she was still the "beautiful girl" he had told his brother Peter about nearly three decades earlier. He remembered telling Peter that the twelve-and-a-half years difference in their ages didn't matter "especially with children in mind." That seemed like such a cruel thought now, after all they had lived through.

But today was a celebration; and Otis pushed such reflection from his mind.

"Ready?" he said, opening the door for his wife.

"You go on in. I want to video the outside of the church," Mary responded.

Mary had just gotten the camera a few months earlier. It was a Sony, chosen only after Otis had conducted enough research to make an informed decision. That was his way. He never made a rash decision, even when buying the smallest items. One year, early in their marriage Mary had wanted a hair dryer. He had studied the various brands, preparing to buy her one for Christmas. Her parents decided they wanted to get the dryer for her, so he had passed along all he had learned about them.

As with most things Mary didn't understand, she wanted to master the camcorder, a most fascinating new toy. She spent hours playing with it: one shade of lettering, then another, outside, inside, buses roaring past their brick home in the Spring Branch section of Houston, their dogs running around the compact, fenced-in backyard.

She filmed Otis at work around the house, sprucing up for the anniversary celebration. Wearing tattered, paint-splattered work clothes, he posed patiently, smiling in that gentle way he had.

"A good-looking man looks good in anything he wears," Mary said, chuckling.

Virtually no one else in the world considered Otis Coulson good-looking. He was nearly bald, painfully thin and hobbled around on a knee debilitated by arthritis. But to Mary he quite literally was her knight in shining armor. He had rescued her from a life of loneliness. Even now, she often talked of him as "dear, sweet Otis" and wondered just what she would do if she ever lost him.

The Coulsons had just completed a fairly major renovation of their three-bedroom ranch. They had painted most of the rooms, laid linoleum in the kitchen and hired workers to put shingles on the roof. The house had been their home for nineteen years, but now they wanted to move to one of the new subdivisions rising on the outskirts of the sprawling city. It seemed odd to some that at their ages—Mary was fifty-four, Otis sixty-six—they had decided to move. But Mary saw their neighborhood as declining, and she wanted out. She was also ready for something new, a departure from the past and the mixed memories of time spent in the house.

Standing now outside the church that had been central to their lives for so many years, Mary hoisted the camera to her shoulder and turned it on. "The 20th of June, 1992, Mary and Otis Coulson's wedding anniversary celebration," she said. She didn't want to miss any aspect of the day. She intended to play it for her parents in Knoxville, Tennessee. Nearly ninety, they tended to stay close to home.

"It's a warm, warm day at St. Francis," she said, thinking how glad she was she had made a short-sleeved, lightweight dress for the occasion. She focused on the outside of the lushly landscaped, beige brick church and its parking lot.

Pleased with her work, Mary strolled inside as the guests started to arrive and stood with Otis in the vestibule. Their eldest daughter, Robin, who had followed in her car, stood beside her dad. She had been at the house since early morning, getting ready for the reception to follow. Mary wanted everything to be perfect. The women had spent two days preparing platters of food, home-baked biscuits and meat, fruit and green salad. Mary had labelled all the different types of cheeses and placed them carefully on a silver tray. She had told Robin to be sure to use the cheese slicer Bob, the middle child, had given her for Christmas. She was so proud he had given her a gift. He usually didn't. In fact, he rarely seemed to give Mary any thought at all.

Robin was different. She tried hard to please her parents, as if to make up for her many goof-ups while she was growing up. She finally had succeeded in making her parents proud the year before when she married Rick Wentworth, who had just gone to work as a jailer at the Harris County Jail. He yearned to become a sheriff's deputy. Mary and Otis believed Robin, twenty-five, lucky to have found Rick. She had had so many boyfriends throughout her teen years and early twenties, so many of them poor choices, Mary had often told her. Rick helped stabilize Robin, to keep her moodiness, her flightiness, in check.

How changed Robin seemed now, especially compared with her parents last "landmark" anniversary; the 20th, when Robin had announced that she was pregnant with her boyfriend's baby. She had sat on the den couch and said without emotion that they were not ready for a baby.

"I am devastated," Mary had told Robin. "I can't believe how lightly you decide not to have this child."

Robin had looked down at the floor, embarrassed,

humiliated. After a long silence, she had asked her parents to pay for the abortion.

"We will not!" Mary had exclaimed. "You'll have to use the money you've saved for a car."

Later, Mary had written in her journal, "Another child to weep for!" Mary's diaries served as an outlet for her, a way to think through life's challenges. She set to paper thoughts and feelings she would never share with anyone. Mary kept the diaries in a green tin box in her closet, and even her closest relatives did not know they existed. She wasn't as faithful with writing in her diaries as she was with church attendance or writing music with her friend Maggi Tucker. Sometimes years passed without a single entry, and then suddenly Mary would write every day, particularly when she faced a problem with her children.

Now, in mid-1992, it was Sarah, the youngest child at twenty-one, who caused the unhappiness. Arriving alone for the service, Sarah wore an attractive beige blazer over a brown-print dress, her long dark hair pulled back in a ponytail. The heavy cast on her left leg looked decidedly out of place with the conservative look of her outfit. Sarah had broken the long bone in her foot a few weeks earlier. Her mother thought she looked beautiful, a nice change from the unkempt hippie look she sometimes sported.

Not too long before the ceremony began, Bob strutted into the church like a chief executive officer at a board meeting. Tall and thin with a sharp angular face, he had the good looks of a department-store model. He kept his reddish hair cropped close and perfectly coiffed. His shirt, beneath a gray suit, was starched; his red tie knotted impeccably. He stood ramrod straight as the service began, two rows back from his parents. Robin sat right behind her parents; Sarah chose a pew on the other side of the church. A handful of others filtered in, including Joe and Barbara Dove. The Doves had been friends of the Coulsons longer than either couple could remember. They had met during the Coulsons' days in Corpus Christi, where the Doves lived still. They knew Otis first, and had met Mary shortly after the Coulsons were married in Knoxville, Tennessee. Mary liked to joke that they were truly ecumenical, having been married in a Methodist Church by a Presbyterian minister. With an easy smile and cheerful voice, Barbara seemed the consummate fourth-grade teacher. She led her husband, a certified public accountant, into the church and sat down beside Bob. She said later, "I'm always for the underdog. When we go to weddings I always ask to sit on the side with the least amount of people. Bob was sitting there by himself." She thought he seemed sullen. When she had seen him several months earlier, Barbara had noticed how much Bob had bulked up. He resembled a weight lifter.

She had told Mary, "His shoulders and arms are so form-fitting. I can't believe he's not working."

Always ready to give her son the benefit of the doubt, Mary had risen to his defense. "Well, the doctor has not released him since his knee injury," she had said, referring to a torn ligament he had suffered playing volleyball more than a year earlier. He still received disability payments from his employer, Ozarka Drinking Water Company, for whom he had delivered bottled water.

Inside St. Francis, the strains of the majestic pipe organ resonated under the steady hands of Maggi

Tucker, Mary's song-writing partner. It was just as Mary hoped it would be. The Reverend Stuart Hoke offered communion for their friends and, reading from the Episcopal Book of Common Prayer, blessed the Coulsons' long marriage. After the hour-long service finished, Mary turned and noticed tears in Sarah's eyes. Always the sweetest, she thought. The family paused for pictures at the altar. Beaming, Mary and Otis were encircled by their children. Bob stood just slightly, almost imperceptibly, apart.

On the way home, Mary said, "I'm so excited about how it was. It was beautiful."

Chapter Ten

The prairie lands of west Texas spread out as flat and stark as a rough-hewn tabletop. For miles, travelers on Interstate 20 see the tall buildings of Midlands looming in the distance. The city seems a mirage, as if the road will never get there. Midlands, Texas, stands as a shrine to the oil business which brought prosperity to a territory that once sprouted only cattle. Midlands and its brutish neighbor Odessa, twenty miles southwest, rise from the Permian Basin. Some 280 million years ago, the 250-by-300-mile basin was an ocean. When it dried up, the plants and animals decayed to form one of the largest pools of oil and gas in the continental United States. The vast oil fields were discovered in the 1920s, making millionaires of ranchers and bringing in the great oil companies as surely as blue jays flock to a thistle feeder. By the 1950s, when Otis Coulson moved to Midlands, the area was a haven for geologists like him, young men eager to make a mark in the oil business. With master's and bachelor's degrees in geology from the University of Arizona and five years experience with the Atlantic Richfield Company, Coulson was fast becoming a specialist in locating oil. What he couldn't locate was a wife. The old saying, "Nice guys finish last" was not wasted on him. He was too nice a guy. Midlands and Odessa were men's towns, full of oil derrick workers, carpenters and riggers. The few women he did meet wanted to be his buddies, not his bride.

After more than a decade in Midlands, Otis met, quite literally, the woman of his dreams. A fellow ARCO geologist, Bob Parke, who also was teaching a geology course at Odessa College, arranged the blind date with a music teacher from the college, Mary Haydn McEver. He told her, "I have someone I want you to meet." She was skeptical, but as was her nature, interested. A few weeks before Christmas 1966, Parke and his wife Mary invited Otis and Mary for dinner. At forty-one, Otis had never found anyone suitable, and at twenty-eight, Mary had found too many who were unsuitable. They were opposites. Otis Coulson was quiet, reflective, with a scientist's mind for analyzing and planning. His income was just over $11,000, and, with the year coming to an end, he could effectively account for most of it. A sizeable portion moved straight into his already burgeoning savings account.

Mary McEver was no planner. Spontaneous and effusive, she delighted in people. She had a way of making those she had just met feel as if they were the most interesting folks she'd ever run across. Naturally curious, she would present some interesting tidbit and then snatch some new information from others. That night at the Parkes', Otis and Mary knew their long days of solitude had ended. Barely a month later, Mary told her parents she was in love.

"Otis is a good man, a good, solid man, who is sweet and considerate and has the loveliest manners you've seen anywhere lately," Mary told them. "And he's happy in his work and does it well because he knows exactly who he is!"

Otis wrote to his younger brother Peter, a theater professor in Wisconsin, "I'm madly, head-over-heels in love with Mary." Ever reflective, Otis said he considered a marriage to Mary "a good match." They were both from the South. He spent his boyhood moving across Georgia and the Carolinas with his father, a construction superintendent. She grew up a banker's daughter in Tennessee. They shared interests: music, travel, books.

"Both of us wanted so badly to be loved and wanted by another . . . and now we are!" he said.

Shortly after they met, Otis was transferred across the state to Corpus Christi. They talked for hours on ARCO's WATTS line, planning a future. Six months later, they were married in Knoxville, Tennessee, in a ceremony steeped in tradition. Mary carried the same sixpence as her older sister, Sarah, and a four-leaf clover supplied by her seven-year-old niece and namesake Linda Mary Danner. Leaving the church for a honeymoon in the Great Smoky Mountains, the Coulsons were so giddy, Otis drove his car into a small ditch. All they could do was laugh as he swung the car back to the pavement. It was such a promising start to a life that would go so far awry.

* * *

The house was cedar-shakes gray with a tidy little yard on Naples Street in Corpus Christi, Texas. Three bedrooms, a bath, barely more than 1,000 square feet, it wasn't much to look at. It was the kind of house most young couples of the 1960s started out in, but for Mary and Otis Coulson it represented stability, the American dream. Such a tranquil, settled life was more than they expected they would have. They returned to Corpus Christi after a honeymoon in the Great Smoky Mountains and two elegant nights at the Royal Orleans Hotel in New Orleans' French Quarter. Returning to box upon box of Otis' things stacked in nearly every room, the Coulsons set up housekeeping with Otis' longtime pal, his dachshund, Max. Mary's belongings arrived from Odessa, Texas, the next week, adding to the jumble that eventually took months to organize. The house took on the hue of home when they carefully positioned the priceless furniture Mary's father, Richard McEver, had made for her through the years.

Situated on the Gulf of Mexico, Corpus Christi offered new possibilities to Mary Coulson. She and Otis often walked along the two-mile-long seawall, a monument to man's constant struggle with the sea, which had been built the decade before and designed by Gutzon Borglum, Mount Rushmore's sculptor. She enjoyed the Art Center and met new friends, among them Barbara Dove, who they were both surprised to learn had attended Gulf Park College in Mississippi some years before Mary was employed there as a music instructor.

Barbara and Mary had long talks and the Doves and the Coulsons frequently met over dinner. Sangria and nachos, sherried meatballs over buttered noodles, Mary loved to cook for her friends. She told Barbara: "Otis is the kindest and most polite man; he even says 'yes ma'am' in bed. That is *too* much."

Shy Otis joined the Toastmaster's Club to improve his speaking skills. The Coulsons joined St. Bartholomew's Episcopal Church, but didn't stay long because other churches hearing Mary's lilting soprano voice began vying for her services. First United Methodist paid her to sing in their choir. She did not let her master's degree in music from Northwestern University in Evaston, Illinois, go to waste. She tutored college students in voice one day each week.

Thinking back on those days, Barbara Dove said, "Thirty years ago, we all felt like you got married and had kids." Mary Coulson wanted nothing else. She dreamed of a large family like her sister Sarah, seven years older than she. At twenty-one, Sarah had married Bob Danner, a man she'd known since her junior high school algebra class. By the time Mary and Otis married, the Danners had five children, ranging in age from five to thirteen. They lived in Chattanooga, Tennessee, ninety miles from the grandparents, and, in Mary's eyes, served as the perfect example of domestic bliss. Sarah wrote long letters to her sister, detailing her frenzied life. Occasionally they recorded messages to each other, a more personal way to strengthen their bonds.

By their third anniversary, the Coulsons remained childless. Surgery on Mary's fallopian tubes did not solve the problem; further tests did not reveal it. One doctor hinted that Mary's weight was the problem. It was a cruel comment to a woman who had battled fat all her life. Mary thought back to the third grade when, humiliated by her ninety-eight pounds, she had had to change to a bigger desk to accommodate her size. She couldn't buy clothes to fit her; her mother had made them all.

On July 15, 1970, the Coulsons initiated adoption proceedings. At the Nueces County Child Welfare Office, they and three other couples were told the ins and outs of adoption. The one piece of information that stuck with Mary Coulson was that it usually took three months to rise to the top of the list to get a baby.

"I think it will be sooner," she told her mother, Bertha McEver. "But we aren't counting on anything."

She also told her mother they had submitted their completed application the very next morning. Anxious for a child?

"Absolutely," said Mary, who laughed about the questions they were asked. "Everything about us, except when we last cut our toenails!"

Mary worried slightly they would be eliminated by the department's age limits, thirty-five for the mother and forty for the father. Mary was thirty-two, but Otis was forty-four.

"Their main concern was that the baby pretty well be assured of both parents until it was grown," Mary told her mother. "But we hope the age thing won't matter because Otis' health is excellent."

Always the optimist, Mary told her father to get busy on a cradle for his sixth grandchild.

They were told they would have only a day's notice that a child was available, so Mary got to work on a nursery, a tricky proposition because like most mothers of that day she did not know whether the baby would be a boy or a girl. Mary scoured the town for suitable material for curtains, finally settling on white percale, edged with rainbow-colored tassels. She stayed up late into the night, sewing. Also in place was the cradle from "Dicko," the name Richard McEver's older grandchildren had bestowed on him years earlier.

Sarah sent words of encouragement and sound advice.

"The best thing I can tell you is keep your perspective," she said. "You all have had plenty of time to think about it and get ready to do a good job, but don't get too anxious, you'll lose your cool. Love, consistency and recognition of the needs of the child and the parent are probably the most important factors in raising children."

In a letter, Sarah wrote to Mary, "A long time ago, when I had the time and the need to think deep thoughts on the objectives of our adventure in parenthood, I came to the conclusion that in reality we had three goals: to guide our children toward their living in a satisfying relationship with God, with themselves and with other people. And in that order."

Mary told her, "If we can be half as good parents to our children as our parents were to us and you and Bob are to your children, we'll do pretty well by them."

Summer flowed to fall and fall to winter before the Coulsons heard the news they prayed for each night. A baby girl was theirs. On February 25, 1971, two-day-old Sarah Lucinda Coulson arrived on Naples Street. The Coulsons were told Sarah's birth mother was a teenager from a good family. She was musical, a trait which stirred Mary's soul. Music centered Mary's life, and her daughter would learn the magic of music, too, learn that music touched places in people as nothing else could. Mary was already planning piano lessons for the child.

"It was just glorious," Barbara Dove said remembering the day the Coulsons brought Sarah home.

"Having Sarah has added a whole new dimension in our lives," Mary told her sister.

"Yes, indeed. Diapers . . . baby food . . . bills," Sarah said, chuckling.

"That too, but it's such a joy to watch her change every day and to see her become more and more aware of the world around her. That feeling when she smiles and you don't expect it! Having Sarah to love brings everything into focus."

Otis shot frame after frame of little Sarah, developing the film himself in his home darkroom. One night he toiled until quarter to two printing pictures of his daughter.

"Richly worth it," he told his brother Peter, who by then was teaching theater at Southwestern Texas State University in San Marcos, Texas, about a three-hour drive away.

On November 5th, the Coulsons arrived at the Nueces County Courthouse for the seven-minute hearing that would make Sarah legally theirs. Their lawyer cautioned them against bringing Sarah, now a crawling, patty-cake-playing nine-month old.

"The courthouse is none too clean a place to take your baby!" the lawyer said. Another couple who started adoption proceedings at the same time as the Coulsons had their son with them.

Mary felt slightly vexed that Otis was asked to answer all the questions and to sign the forms for Sarah's new birth certificate.

"It certainly gave me the impression that Otis was the only one who mattered in this family," she told her mother. "Oh, well, the important thing is that everything went off without a hitch."

That night, the Doves and their two-year-old son Todd went to the Coulsons to celebrate. They shared a bottle of Cold Duck. Mary told Barbara she knew that now she would get pregnant.

"You adopt a lovely child and then you're pregnant," said Mary. "It happens all the time."

Chapter Eleven

They looked like the children on the Campbell's Soup cans. Round faces, pudgy cheeks, red hair, Robin and Bobby radiated the kind of All-American charm any parent would flaunt. But 1971 had been a particularly bad year for the children's mother, and all she could think of as the year plodded toward its final weeks, was getting rid of them. Robin was four, Bobby three.

Jostling a small bag containing the children's clothes, she pushed open the heavy doors to the Mann Building, an aged, three-story, brick structure near the center of downtown Corpus Christi, Texas. She was only twenty-two, but looked older, with a peculiar confused look about her even on her rare good days. Edging close to the building directory, she located the office she was seeking—the Nueces County Child Welfare Department—and headed for the second floor.

Down a long hallway, she tugged at her children, scolding them to keep up. She was in a hurry.

"I can't take care of these children anymore," she said to a woman seated behind a small wooden desk.

"Yes, ma'am," the woman said, and motioned for her to sit down while she located a social worker. The woman and her children were shown into an office about the size of a small bedroom. On the wall behind the desk hung a corkboard full of pictures of children, dozens and dozens of them, forming a collage of smiling faces.

"I want you to find my children another family," the mother said firmly, her eyes cast downward to avoid looking at the woman behind the desk. "And I need to go. Can you take them now?"

June Randall was only two years older than the children's mother. She had worked at the welfare agency for slightly more than a year, and already she had placed seventy-five children in new homes. The situation facing her now was nothing new. Lost jobs, lost loves, lost lives, it all figured in. About every week a mother decided to turn her child over to the state. Most were babies, but a few were older children like Robin and Bobby. Neglected, unwanted, sometimes abused sexually and physically, the older children were the hardest to place. June looked at the two children before her, whimpering now as they realized their mother was about to leave them.

First, June thought, she would get what information she could. Then, she would try to convince the mother to keep her children.

The children's father was in Rhode Island, the mother said vacantly. That was her home, too. She had been in Texas just a few months.

"Where were the children born?" June asked.

"Kingston, Rhode Island." She gave Robin's birthday as February 1967 and Bob's as March 11, 1968.

"How much did they weigh?"

The mother looked at her like she was speaking a foreign language.

"I just can't remember," she said finally. "I don't know. I don't have any more information."

Although June knew there was more to tell, she also knew instinctively the woman had finished talking. June told her the agency would do all it could to help her, financial assistance, counseling. She had choices; giving up her children was not the answer.

"The agency will even place the children in a foster home while you get on your feet," June implored.

The woman would not be moved.

"I need to get going," she responded firmly. "Where are the papers I need to sign?"

Mary and Otis settled easily into their new world as parents of Sarah. As with most parents, they relished every achievement, noting it in the family letters Mary sent to the far-flung families, Otis's parents in Tucson, her sister, now in Florence, South Carolina, and her parents in Knoxville. Mary and her sister traded tape recordings, with Sarah offering more child care advice, some appreciated, some not.

As the days passed and baby Sarah crawled and talked and walked, no baby joined her. Otis and Mary contacted the welfare agency once again. Peggy Mercer, a caseworker, told them it was unlikely they would be able to adopt another baby any time soon. There were many would-be parents but few babies.

As the Texas heat beat down on the city in the summer of 1972, Peggy Mercer called Mary.

"I was wondering if you would consider an older child," Peggy said.

"What do you mean?" Mary asked.

"We have two children, a brother and sister, three and four, who were abandoned by their mother. They've been in a foster home for about eight months. The boy is very angry but the girl is much more passive. She cries a lot."

The Coulsons' names had come up that day at a meeting of the caseworkers, and all agreed, an older stable couple like them would be just what the children needed. The Coulsons home study, prepared when they adopted Sarah, described them as a loving couple with good communication skills.

"I looked for the bad and found only good," Mercer told her coworkers.

Mary and Otis talked about the idea that night and agreed to at least see the children. They went the next day. Peggy took the children to play at the T-heads, the parks on the bay built with dirt scooped from the shoreline when Corpus Christi's seawall was constructed. The arrangement was perfect; Otis and Mary could see the children, without feeling any pressure about whether they would take them or not. The children didn't even know they were being observed.

The Coulsons came upon the trio as they were feeding gulls near the water's edge.

"They are so cute," Mary exclaimed to Otis, who looked on with his characteristic smile. But he was not as moved by the sight as his wife. To Mary, the children were the essence of her dreams. She had especially wanted a son. How could a mother simply get rid of her children like a sack of unwanted kittens? It was more than Mary could bear to think about.

That night, they talked about adopting the children, a proposal that seemed to come to them from nowhere, completely unexpected. An instant family; could it be fate or God working in their lives? To go from being two to five in one year seemed delightfully impossible.

"What about abuse?" Otis wondered.

"That causes me to want to help them more," Mary said. "What chance have they had at a normal life? We have so much to give. Remember, my darling, Otis, love can conquer all."

But Mary's mother and sister were against it. Did she realize how much more work it would be?

"Buying one pair of shoes is much different from three," the usually steady Sarah said in a long-distance call, her brood roaring in the background. Mary felt like she had so many times before, like the little sister who somehow simply couldn't find her way.

That night, Otis and Mary decided to let the children come to their home for a visit. It went well. Over the next weeks, the children visited several times, and the Coulsons prayed about what they should do. Finally, in late July, they gave Peggy Mercer the word.

"We want them," they said.

On July 31st, Otis came home from work about 11:00 A.M., just ahead of Peggy Mercer with Robin and Bobby in tow. Bobby raced up the walkway, knocked briskly and threw his arms around Mary's neck when she opened the door. Robin, a bit more reticent, tagged along behind younger brother Bobby, exploring the house. Sarah came up behind them both.

The Coulsons bought Bobby a Fisher-Price airplane and Robin the Stuffin's family puppet and showed them the bunk beds they would sleep in if they decided they wanted to live there. They met Max the dog.

The next day, Robin and Bobby moved in for good.

They brought with them all their belongings: two boxes of clothes too small, too used. Bobby wore his only pair of shoes, sandals, which had worn blisters in his heels. Robin's only shoes were patent leather, the kind little girls wear to church. Her dresses were at least a size too small. Bobby's clothes were torn and stained.

They celebrated the children's arrival with a picnic in the park near Otis' office at ARCO. Bobby and Robin spent their first night at the Coulsons in peace. They drifted off to unfettered sleep and slept without a stir the entire night.

Mary assembled special scrapbooks for the children. Bob's was called *A Book All About a Little Boy Named Bobby*. The books included a photograph of the children's real mother and one of Margie Salinas, who was Robin and Bobby's foster mother for a year. Margie had four children of her own, including a son who was adopted.

Mary hoped the books would help the children to know that they were wanted and that the adoption was permanent. The Coulsons would be there no matter what.

The children had wished desperately for a puppy, and Mary and Otis bought a daschund and named him Hans.

When Bobby saw the picture of his biological mother

in his scrapbook, he ripped it from the page. Furiously, he tore it in dozens of tiny pieces.

He never wanted to see her again.

Mary knew little about the parents, only that the mother had dropped the children at the welfare office a few weeks before Christmas last year. That was as much as Mary cared to know. She still couldn't understand how a mother could simply give up her children. She wanted her own child so urgently and here was someone who could throw them off like old clothes to Goodwill. Mary was determined to make it right for these pitiful children who, until now, had no hope for a good life. She would see that they had clean, sturdy clothes, a good education and a sense of right and wrong. God would center their lives. In fact, she immediately made plans to have them baptized. She also took them for their first portraits.

On their second day at the Coulsons, the family rose early, around six, and gulped a breakfast of doughnuts and milk.

"Not too nutritional, but it is appetizing and I see well-received," Mary said, smiling as she looked around at the table full of little faces. "Let's load up. We need to put Daddy on a wild red plane to fly into the wild blue yonder."

Later, Peggy Mercer came by just as Mary was putting the children down for naps. Sitting on the edge of the bed, Mary sang softly, her sweet tones soothing even Peggy.

She reported back to her colleagues that afternoon: "The Coulsons are the most wonderful people I've ever met. Mary is such an intriguing person, so assured and smart. You ought to hear her sing."

Later, with Otis gone for the night on a business trip, Mary gathered the children on her bed for their nightly prayers. She placed a picture of Otis in his usual spot.

"He's not coming back," Bobby blurted out, tears streaming from his eyes. "I know it, he's not coming back."

Mary hugged him and said softly, "Of course he's coming back." Bobby stiffly pushed her away. That was not what he knew. People didn't come back in his life.

Chapter Twelve

Rumors of transfers flew through the ARCO office in Corpus Christi as steadily as kites in a March wind. Every time Mary Coulson heard a new one about her husband, she cringed. Geologists move around like felons dodging the police. She knew that when she married Otis Coulson, but the company could literally move them anywhere in the world. Alaska was the place Mary feared most of all.

Mary liked her life in Corpus Christi. It was where she came to live as a young bride, where she found and adopted her children. She had devoted friends. Every day, Mary and Barbara Dove talked on the phone like schoolgirls or saw each other.

In 1973, six years after they moved to Corpus Christi, Otis came home and announced he had gotten a transfer to the Houston office. Houston. Mary felt a sense of relief. She didn't want to move, but Houston was just four hours to the north. It also was a much larger city, brimming with all the cultural amenities Mary could want: the symphony, the opera, world-class art museums.

The Coulsons found a three-bedroom brick ranch on Westview in Houston's growing Spring Branch Woods subdivision. The lot was deep with large oak trees and a patio out back overlooking it all. Mary could imagine starting her days out there in the months of spring— her favorite season—or fall, sipping coffee, watching tiny animals and writing in her journal.

The movers came in mid-July, packing up the assorted remnants of their lives. It was an experience. Where Otis Coulson was an organizer, his wife was a disorganizer. She had more piles of stuff than a writer on deadline. Some sort of project was always under way; crocheting for a niece, cross-stitching for her mother, a dress for a daughter. It wasn't unusual for a guest to sit down on a sewing needle, thrown down absently on the couch.

With the goods packed on a moving van, Mary walked through the empty house. She remembered her days as a new mother when Sarah was a baby and when Robin and Bobby had come to live with them. She could almost see that little red-haired fellow who kept racing out toward busy Naples Drive on his first days there. He felt no fear. Finally, panicked, Mary had walked Bobby to the edge of the road, inches from cars roaring past and said firmly, "You step out on that, you will be a grease spot on the road!" She must have gotten through to him because he didn't do it again. But was that too harsh? she wondered. Mary Coulson was always good at second-guessing herself, especially those swift, impulsive decisions of motherhood.

She walked over to the corner of the living room where they had always positioned the Christmas tree. The first Christmas with Robin and Bobby had been especially exciting for her. She had made lots of plans, baking goodies and buying special presents for the children. She had wanted it to be the best ever. Little Bobby and Robin deserved it. Had they ever had a Christmas of abundance? she had wondered. Her parents had come in from Knoxville, adding to the feeling of family togetherness. On Christmas morning, the children had lunged at their presents. Little Sarah, just two years old, had stood feebly as Robin and Bobby gathered up the boxes with their names on them and horded them in different corners of the room. They had torn into their packages and throughout the day had kept the presents close by. They had refused to share with anyone else, as if the gifts might be taken away.

Patiently and quietly, Mary had wrapped her arms around them and said, "These are yours, darlings. No one will take them from you. They are yours to keep forever, just as we will all be together forever."

This house was also where she and Robin had come to terms with who was the mother. Robin had become her brother's protector in those strange months after their mother had left them and wanted to continue the role when they moved in with the Coulsons. Mary ultimately won, but she had told her parents, it was a true fight for power.

The Coulsons quickly assimilated to life in Houston, thanks largely to the many activities of their children and their church work. Mary volunteered in the elementary school her children attended. Bobby seemed to blossom in that first year in Houston. Once Mary went into his classroom with another mother and watched for an hour as the children worked quietly and independently, completing one task after another without being told what to do.

The other mother said to Mary, "I can't help but think of all the times I've told my child at home to *Do Something!*"

They laughed and Mary knew exactly what she meant.

The Coulsons were regulars at the opera, attending the premiere of an opera based on Chekhov's play *The Seagull* and *Le Nozze di Figaro* in early 1974. Mary loved all types of music, but especially opera. A favorite gift was an album of opera.

Not long after the Coulsons moved onto Westview Street, their son brought home a neighbor from across the street, Andy Tucker. He was two years older than Bobby, but they quickly became pals, playing softball in the yard or sleeping over at each other's house. Through that friendship, Mary met Andy's mother, Maggi. In her, Mary discerned a kindred spirit. Maggi was the minister of music at First Congregational Church of Houston, where her husband, Bob, was the senior minister. Maggi had received a bachelor's degree in organ from the American Conservatory of Music and a master's degree in choral conducting from the University of Houston. Mary had a bachelor's in music from Maryville College in Tennessee and a master's from Northwestern University in Evanston, Illinois. Soon, they shared in performance their love of music. Mary occasionally sang solos at the Tuckers' church. Sometimes they set up a recorder and taped Mary singing with accompaniment by Maggi on the organ. Eventually, the women started writing anthems for children's choirs together.

"We'll try this once and if it doesn't work, it's not worth losing a friendship over," Maggi told her.

She agreed. Mary wrote the words and Maggi set them to music. It was the perfect union. Everything they wrote was published; the first, *Song of Creation*, came out in 1985. Maggi considered it perfect for children, not trite, but playful with a deep theological meaning.

Mary's verses were about God making all the animals, including enormous whales, tiny ants and sleek, fat seals. The song ended with God creating her, and though she wasn't too sure where she should go, she was sure that when God finished her, He looked at her and called her good.

Prayer for Today was published in 1986 and sold well. The next year, Mary received a royalty check for $666.10 and immediately photocopied it to send to her parents. At the top, she wrote, "Thought you'd like to see this!" She drew a broad-grinned happy face at the end.

Four years after Mary's death, Maggi would say, "Mary wrote sensitive words for children. I still have yet to work with anyone equal to her."

Four years to the day that Bob and Robin first arrived on the doorstep of that little cedar-shake house in Corpus Christi, the family headed for church, just as they did each Sunday. Driving toward St. Francis in the elegant Memorial section of Houston, Mary said a little prayer.

"Please, Lord, on the next occasion of this anniversary, make me happier and more content."

Mary's life had become a seemingly endless round of swimming lessons for Bob, dance lessons for Sarah, Girl Scouts, Boy Scouts. Robin was nine, Bob eight, and

Sarah, five. On the outside, Mary mimicked the lives of other mothers, but behind the doors her life was controlled by a child of anger. Sometimes she thought she could almost see it raging and rolling inside Bob. He pushed the limits harder than a test pilot going for a world record. Around adults, he took on a different persona, the ever polite and gracious child.

A neighbor told Mary, "He is much more polite than the other children." Mary relished the praise, but knew too well the other temperament lurking just below the surface. There always seemed to be so much tension, Mary thought.

That afternoon, she snuck off to the Museum of Fine Arts.

"I need to restore my soul," she told Otis, sounding a tad melodramatic. But melodrama was her life. She was creative to the core, singing herself to sleep when she was just barely old enough to talk. When she was three, her parents had paid to record her singing.

Sitting in the quiet of the museum, Mary thought about something a fellow church member said that morning.

"We should storm heaven, besiege God for an answer to our prayers and be ready for a no."

"I've done that," Mary thought. "Everything just goes on. Perhaps God is telling me not to fight the confusion but to create an inner quiet place for myself to go when I need to reflect."

Mary walked through the museum and for some reason an odd thought came to mind.

"Am I going to live long enough to work this out?" she thought, knowing full well her health was excellent.

The extent of her illness through the years were colds and vocal chords strained by singing.

Also troubling to her was Bob's apparent inability to tell the truth. On a trip to Knoxville to visit his grandparents that summer, he had leaped up and caught hold of a branch of a pecan tree. Swinging happily, the limb had snapped and hung limply in the yard. His grandfather, Dicko, had called out, "What happened to that limb?"

Bob had hastily replied, "I don't know. I didn't do it."

Dicko had chortled to his wife, "There is no difference between a lie and the truth to that boy."

The Coulsons returned to Knoxville for Christmas. Otis and Mary were ready for a quiet, family time. A month earlier, they had feared Mary was pregnant. At thirty-eight, with three children, all troublesome in some fashion, a baby was the last thing on her Christmas list. For years, she had prayed for a baby. Now she prayed against one.

"The child might be born defective," she told Otis. "I'm afraid. Just when I feel I'm getting on top of things, it gets bad again."

But the worries were unfounded. A baby was not to be. They headed off to Knoxville and celebrated Otis' fifty-first birthday the day before Christmas with Bob and Sarah nursing fevers and possibly strep throat.

"Turn off the Christmas music," Bob demanded as Mary and her mother worked in the kitchen, preparing the next day's feast.

"You know, just before Christmas, I always get depressed," Bertha McEver said. "I don't really understand why."

Mary thought about being at home, in the house where she grew up. So many memories. It was a mixed metaphor for her, too, to be here.

"Life is not primary colors," she told her mother. "It's shaded and mixed and joined colors that sometimes don't look so good together. I haven't learned to love the subtle."

"Turn off the Christmas music," Bob said again but louder this time.

Mary refused. Suddenly it occurred to her that Bobby was always more ornery and difficult at Christmastime. That was the season of abandonment, when his biological mother had left him at the welfare office.

The next morning he woke at 3:40 A.M. and immediately woke his sisters and everyone else in the house.

"Why are you waking everyone up at this hour?" Mary asked, unhappy with only an hour's sleep. "This is ridiculous. It is the middle of the night. Can't you be more considerate? Think of other people from time to time."

They all got up, though, and opened presents. The girls had made many cute little items for the house, including a napkin holder. Bob gave her nothing. She couldn't believe he would just forget her like that.

In February, Mary and Otis decided that Bob needed professional help. They took him to a counselor, a woman named Joanne Tangedahl. Almost immediately, they began to see some progress with Bob. He seemed less angry. The counselor told Mary that Bob seemed particularly in tune with group vibes. He started to connect to the family more. One evening Otis was surprised when Bob asked him for a back rub.

"A little at a time," she told her husband in bed that night.

Late in her life, Mary Coulson would say the only time each member of her family enjoyed doing something together was the spring they went to Europe. Mary loved to travel, yet most of her journeys were simple trips to see her parents or sister. Often, she felt envious of friends who ventured to far-flung corners of the world. But even though her husband loved to travel, too, he loved not spending money more. Friends wanting to be nice called him "conservative" with money; others called him tight. Money truly was the only place where Mary and Otis rubbed against each other. Mary simply could not manage it. When she was in college, her father set up a checking account for her at his bank in Knoxville. He had done the same for his older daughter Sarah and she ended each year with money left over. The first month Mary was at Maryville, she was over-drawn.

Otis knew this about his wife, and he was a realist. He was twelve years older than she, and men live shorter lives than women. He knew she faced many years without him. He wanted to be absolutely sure she had the money she needed to live comfortably for the rest of her life, so he invested carefully and grew a nest egg.

In 1980, Otis decided the time was right to take the trip Mary had dreamed of for so long. They flew from Houston to Atlanta on May 12, 1980, and then across the Atlantic to Gatwick Airport. They had arranged for a flat in Streatham.

The Coulsons saw it all: Queen Mary's Doll House,

the Jewel Room, Windsor Palace, London Zoo. They took the children to Greenwich to see the Old Royal Observatory. Chagrined, Mary noticed women had to pay to use public toilets, men didn't.

"Chauvinists," she said.

At thirteen, Robin was particularly aware of the fashions.

"Everyone wears either very high heels or slides," she told her mother.

Bob was surprised that when he ordered a hamburger he was served ground-up ham.

"Not too good," he said.

They spent two days in Walsall with Otis' cousin Fancy Jackson and her husband Arthur before heading on to Scotland. On their first day there, they took a ninety-minute bus trip around Edinburgh.

"I see why people love this city so much," Mary said.

Back in their room, Otis discovered he had been undercharged. While the family rested, Otis went back and paid what he owed. On the receipt the driver wrote, "Thank you for your honesty."

From Edinburgh, they went to York. At St. Mary's Abbey, Mary watched as person after person was turned away from going inside because a service was about to begin. Mary was determined to see the inside of the great church. She stood up to the verger and said authoritatively, "We'd like to attend the service."

He quickly moved the rope and stood aside as all five Coulsons promenaded to their seats. Choir boys in red robes with ruffles at the neck sang angelically. The organ reverberated.

"I am so glad we went to church," she said as they left.

They moved on to Wales, to Llanduduo and Cardiff, where they stayed with more cousins, David and Allison Jackson. David taught German at the University of Cardiff. Bob was intrigued by David's "allotment," a small plot of land where he grew vegetables. Bob helped out a day or two. Finally on May 31st, they went back to London for their trip home.

Chapter Thirteen

Two weeks after Bob Coulson's sixteenth birthday, his mother remarked that she was always amazed when Bob was agreeable. In her heart of hearts, she always expected him to be difficult."

He seemed to her like fingernails scraping a blackboard. His room was a constant mess. He flitted in and out of the house like a boarder. When he was home he usually remained behind the locked door of his room. He left notes, chastising her for buying the wrong food. "I only eat certain food, it seems you could buy it," said a note he left for her on the kitchen counter.

"It is so scary to me," she told Otis. "He has such a resistance to authority. Sometimes I have a terrible fear—no focus but sorrow and anger. Why can't he quit fighting and get on with living?"

Her husband could only shrug. He didn't know the answer either. They had given Bob all they knew to give.

They saw his anger and took him to counseling until he refused to go any longer. They gave him cornet lessons and he played well enough to join the high school band. He played soccer and was a Boy Scout. But some problem usually arose with every pursuit. He quit Boy Scouts, telling his father the scoutmaster had it in for him and wouldn't let him attain the highest honor, Eagle Scout.

"What's the point?" he said.

He treated his parents like he was ashamed of them. His father was a "wimp," his mother "obese." He preferred hanging around his friend Scott Smith's father, who worked on cars and showed Bob all he knew. A nice-looking man, Mike Scott had the well-pressed look of a man about town. He wore tailored trousers and expensive cowboy boots. He worked as a civil engineer and was divorced from Scott's mother.

Mary suspected that the older Bob grew, the less contact he would have with the family. And in some measure that was fine with her. A part of her yearned for the day when Bob turned eighteen so she would not have to be legally responsible for him. Another part wept for the precious little red-haired boy she never really had.

"It will take an effort to keep him part of the group, an effort I may make but one frankly I will make reluctantly," Mary vowed.

A month after his sixteenth birthday, he took a job at the Paradise Bakery. Three days later, he brought home some leftover pastries.

"I don't mind if you have some but I want them here when I want them," he said to Mary as he glared at her through distant eyes. The slights continued. A couple of weeks later, he brought home pink roses left from a wedding the bakery catered.

"I'm going to put these in the refrigerator, okay?" he asked Mary. "I'll probably take them to somebody tomorrow."

Mary never knew who he gave them to, but she certainly knew it wasn't her, the mother who took him in when no one else wanted him.

"Sometimes it seems to me that the last time Bob gave us anything freely was the hug he gave us the first time we met!" she told Otis.

On Mother's Day, Bob surprised Mary with a new journal of burgundy corduroy, with a ribbon to mark a certain place in the book. It was the nicest journal she'd ever had. The others were thin, inexpensive models. It was such a thoughtful gesture, but he did it with such nonchalance, as if it didn't matter to him one way or another whether she had a good Mother's Day. He didn't pay her any attention after saying, "Happy Mother's Day" and handing over the journal. Robin, on the other hand, worked hard to make the day special. She and Mary munched popcorn while watching *Jubilee Trail*, a Forest Tucker movie.

"Robin is a good and loving daughter," she told Otis, adding that she felt as angry with Bob as she felt happy with Robin.

"I don't even want to start writing in the journal he gave me with these feelings," she said.

Five days later, Mary finally opened the handsome book and detailed her day.

* * *

At the end of April in 1985, ARCO announced a major restructuring. Fifty percent of the professional staff would be cut. Many old-timers would qualify for early retirement. Others would simply be laid off.

That evening, Otis Coulson stepped into his kitchen and told his wife the news. She was stunned. He was only fifty-nine and had been with the company for thirty-four years.

"It's not definite who will be offered the incentives," he said.

"I know it will pass," she replied, trying to reassure her husband. She wrapped her arms around his neck and pulled him close. After all these years, Mary Coulson rarely stood near her husband without touching him in some way, patting his arm, holding his hand. She always snuggled close to him in pictures and loved the close feeling of being together, talking in bed.

"It's the loss of the cushion that troubles me," he said.

"What's important is us together," she said. "We've been all right before and we still will."

This was the kindest, most dedicated man in that whole company, Mary thought. How could they throw him out after his devotion, dedication and hard work?

Otis went to his desk and started figuring. It would be a scene Mary would witness often in the coming weeks. Adding and adding again the money they had in savings, certificates, stocks, bonds. The numbers never changed. He just needed the reassurance that they weren't swinging out on a tether from which they could fall.

As the summer glided along, the Coulsons found out that Otis indeed would be offered early retirement with no opportunity to say no. He would get retirement benefits as if he were sixty-five, insurance coverage and payments equalling Social Security. He also could take monthly payments from his pension or a lump sum. He checked with several financial planners and friends and chose the lump sum.

Everyone had an opinion of what to do with it and what he should do with his life.

"Just manage your investments," one friend said.

Mary confided to friends that the prospect of this retirement was truly frightening to her.

"If he is happy and felt productive I wouldn't mind if he were around a lot more," she said. "I love having him nearby and it would be nice to share some of the daytime."

Otis told her, "I'm beginning to be excited about this." As fall neared, Mary could tell his depression was waning.

The retirement was official in mid-September. They hosted a dinner with neighbors Bob and Maggi Tucker to celebrate. Earlier that month, Robin had enrolled as a freshman at Stephen Austin College, Bob had started his senior year at Spring Woods Senior High and Sarah had begun her freshman year at the high school. Changes for everyone.

In October, Otis and Mary packed their car and drove to Florence, South Carolina, to see Mary's sister, Sarah. At fifty-four, Sarah was suffering from cancer and the prognosis was not good. Years earlier, she found a lump in her breast, dutifully had it checked and the results showed it was not malignant. The next year, a large cancerous tumor was found there. By fall of 1985, she was quite ill. She had been through all the cancer protocol, operation, chemotherapy. Her arm, where the lymph nodes had been removed was so swollen she could not use it. The sadness Mary felt for her sister—and for herself at the prospect of losing her—was immeasurable, but she tried to keep it buried. In her characteristic boisterous way, Mary stormed into her sister's white frame house like the Welcome Wagon lady. She sat with Sarah and talked and read aloud. She tried to be helpful but ended up tiring her out.

Two days later, they headed to Knoxville to see Mary's parents.

"I want to demand a miracle of God for Sarah," she told her mother.

Back in Houston, Bob Coulson gathered with his pals, Mike Scott and Scott Smith. Coulson seemed agitated, Smith remembered later.

Coulson had said, "My parents are off spending my inheritance."

Dressed in his cap and gown, tassel hanging over the side of his cap, Bob Coulson looked pleased and proud. His parents felt the same. Getting to this point had been no picnic, but joy was the feeling of the day in May 1986 when he graduated from Spring Woods Senior High. His academic record had been less than impressive. He had failed English in his junior year, but made it up in summer school. He had been caught cheating at one point and his grades were at best average. Yet, Bob earned his highest marks ever in the first semester of his senior year, all B's and C's. His younger sister had a straight-A report card for her freshman year.

Mary suffered a twinge of envy when the honor grads were announced at the graduation exercises, but she did not let on. Instead, she kept trying to remind herself there was more to life than academics. That was a hard lesson for her to learn. Education rested among the highest goals of her life. She and her husband had been honor students throughout their schooling and had earned advanced degrees in their fields. Neither Bob nor Robin had been good students, despite all the help and encouragement Otis and Mary gave through the years. And to make matters worse, Robin had flunked out of college in her first year. Another disappointment, though not as great as when Mary had discovered Robin was sleeping with her boyfriend in high school, but close.

When Robin had come home from college, shamed by her failure, Mary had suddenly realized that where Robin was concerned, she had been living in fantasyland.

"She has simply been saying what we wanted to hear," Mary had told Otis. "For years, she's been doing this!"

They sat in their bedroom, their private enclave where they had spent so many precious moments, alone together, where they had shared their closest thoughts and feelings.

Otis had been as disappointed as she. But Mary had felt betrayal.

"So mixed up with my disappointments and anger is a terrible sense of my own failure," she had said.

"Mary, you have not failed her. She has failed us,"

Otis had replied. Steady, darling Otis, Mary had thought.

Now Bob would be going to college. That offered some consolation. He planned to enroll at Southwest Texas State University, where his uncle Peter taught theater.

In the summer before he left for college, Bob worked two jobs, checking at Randalls Supermarket and concessions at the Loew's movie theater at Town and Country Mall. Bob didn't really like working checkout. He preferred bagging and carrying groceries to people's cars. He charmed the little old ladies like Cary Grant and they always gave him large tips.

It was money in the pocket, surely, easily.

Bob Coulson enrolled at Southwest Texas State and by mid-September was talking about dropping out.

"I hate the dorms," he told his uncle Peter on one of their Sunday afternoon's at Kettle's Restaurant in San Marcos, a popular eating place for the after-church crowd in the college town of 29,000 people. Every now and then, Coulson would meet his uncle at St. Mark's Episcopal Church, where Peter was a member, and the two would go out to eat together. He seldom saw his nephew otherwise.

Years later, Peter remembered, "I pretty much left it up to him if he wanted to communicate. Bob was always on his own so to speak. He seemed to be content and I figured if he wanted to get together, fine."

More than any other relative, Peter knew the Coulson children best. He had lived close by for most of their childhood years and visited every couple of months. A confirmed bachelor, he did not have a natural affinity with children. To be sure, he loved them, but he was not an effusive person. He reminded many people of his older brother, Otis. He had the same methodical ways, planning and carrying out of plans with military precision. Peter travelled often, around the world, to Alaska, Europe, Russia, anywhere the urge struck. He kept detailed records of his trips, which he enjoyed reading years later. Like Otis, he loved photography and often served as the official family photographer for important occasions.

But Bob had always been so distant in all his dealings with family members, so Peter did not want to push himself on his nephew. Sometimes, Peter thought the real reason Bob called was he wanted the lunch.

After his third time he filled his plate from the buffet, Coulson told his uncle the dorms were too loud. He couldn't sleep.

"Somebody's always setting off the fire alarm," he said.

Mary and Otis did not want to hear Bob's talk of coming home.

"It isn't exactly that I don't want him home, but I do so need breathing time," Mary told Otis. "Does it make me a bad parent to want them to get on with their lives?"

As usual, Mary's steady rock Otis said, "Of course not, Mary."

Robin, nineteen, was now living at home, and Sarah, at fifteen, was still in high school. So only Bob was missing, but his absence was enough to cause a distinct shift in the air. No more fights or bickering between Robin and Bob. No more closed-door meetings between

Sarah and Bob in her bedroom. No more coming and going in the wee hours of the mornings. It was calm.

"I love this new order in my house and in my life. I don't know if I can readjust."

Mary told Bob, "Please stay one more semester. You are just getting adjusted there and you will like it after a fashion."

"I'm finally learning to study," he replied. "It will be so much cheaper to go to school and live at home. You won't have to pay room and board."

He told them he planned to take twelve hours at Houston Community College for the spring semester and go back to work at Randall's.

Back in August, when Robin had come home they had set down rules for her. She had to help out around the house and get a job. The family cars would be at her disposal only three times a week. The same applied to Bob. On a steno pad, Mary wrote out the pros and cons of him coming home. There was only one pro: "We have to spend less money on his expenses." There were five arguments against it. Hassle, late hours, mess, food bill, and she and Otis would have less freedom. She also wrote out solutions and set them before Bob as conditions for coming home. He would have to be considerate and help around the house. His parents would give him room and board only, no money. He'd have to earn his own, plus hold down a full class load. He also would have to take out the trash, make his bed and go to church every now and then. They laid it all out for him at Thanksgiving and he agreed.

Reluctantly, Mary and Otis drove to San Marcos to pick Bob up in early December after he had taken his last final.

In the early part of the new year, Bob was named assistant acolyte master at St. Francis Episcopal, an affluent church of about 1,750 members known for reaching out to others less fortunate. The Coulsons had been members there for a decade or more. Bob had been confirmed in the cavernous dark wood and beige brick sanctuary in 1982, when he was fourteen.

Assistant acolyte master was a job normally held by someone much older than Bob, who was not yet nineteen. Like his sisters, he had served the church as an acolyte through his youth, wearing his white robe, walking proudly into the church in front of the priests. As master, his responsibility was to make sure the children knew their different jobs. He taught them how to don their vestments, walk into the church in the procession and what to do at the altar.

"He was very good in public," an active church member remembered years later. "Some would say he was an actor."

Nearly two years after his retirement, Otis Coulson was feeling secure enough with his money situation to surprise his wife with a trip to Europe—three weeks, two in England. It was the off-season so prices were quite reasonable, he told his brother. They could swing it.

They bought their tickets in early February for a trip to begin the next month, March 15, 1987. The day before they left, Mary went to the drug store and bought three similar blank cards. She took them home, sat down at her desk and composed notes to her children.

On the envelope of each card she wrote, "In the event of my death."

She chose a pink card with white flowers for Robin. She filled both sides of the card, beginning with, "There is a special bond between parents and each child—forged by who and what they each are. You are our oldest child and you are special to us because of the uniqueness of yourself. Sometimes, today, I look at the lovely young woman you are and I seem to see again the chubby, five-year-old with the pixie haircut and the big smile sitting on my piano bench with her brother and balloons."

Mary wrote that their relationship had been strained at times, and she had hoped they would have been closer.

"You are not a child of my body, but you have become a child of my heart," she wrote.

Turning to a blue card with a butterfly imprint, Mary wrote to Sarah, "I was not your biological mother but you were part of us from the moment you opened your eyes and looked at us. Your life is just beginning, and it holds much promise and possibility." She reminded her daughter to use her gifts of intelligence, openness and sensitivity.

"What we are is God's gift to us. What we become is our gift to God."

The last card was for Bob. Mary tackled it last because it was the most difficult. She carefully chose words she hoped would inspire him, nudge him toward becoming the caring man she believed he could be. She didn't want to make him angry so that he would lose sight of the meaning.

"At this point in your life, it is often difficult for me

to say and for you to hear some of the necessary things. So, as we leave on this trip, I wanted to put down some of the things I may not get to say myself.

"You are our only son, and hold a special place in our lives. In this past year, you have grown up a great deal and we have been proud of your accomplishments as well as gratified to see you becoming a responsible adult.

"I have a wish for your future. It is that as you continue to mature, you will be more and more able to put aside the 'persona' of being Bob and let more of the real you show through. You have begun to face the world without a mask. Keep it up. When you are not afraid to let people know the vulnerable, loving, fun-loving side of you without hiding it behind the macho-macho, more sarcastic, teasing side, you will find a real contentment.

"Because you were never my baby, there are mother and son things we were never able to share. But I have grown over the years to love you as mothers love children from conception.

"Continue to grow and open yourself to the world. You have much to gain and so much to give. Your Dad and I love you, Mother."

Mary left the cards on the dresser in her bedroom.

On the airplane trip over the Atlantic, Mary turned to Otis and said, "I wish I felt the children would miss us."

At about the same time, Bob Coulson was with his friends Mike Scott and Scott Smith. Bob looked at his watch and said, "Well, the plane must be over the Atlantic right now. It would be a shame if it fell into the ocean."

Chapter Fourteen

The day after Mary Coulson's forty-ninth birthday, she and Bob had it out. The hard feelings had simmered for months. Mary felt he had not lived up to the agreement they had made when he returned home from Southwest Texas State. Regularly he strolled in at two or three in the morning. He barely lifted a finger to help out. Mary felt he treated the house like a hotel.

"You are insensitive to my needs," he said, accusingly. "You're the one who caused all my fucking problems."

Mary was stunned.

"You have no idea how many times we have done for you," she said. "You are totally ungrateful. You think the grass is always greener in someone else's life and you care for no one really, except yourself."

"You are always looking at me funny," he said. "Jesus."

"Your language is totally unacceptable," she countered. But she knew he simply didn't care what she thought. She also knew it made no difference to argue with him. Only he could change his heart.

The next day—Otis and Mary's twentieth wedding anniversary—they learned that Robin was pregnant and planning an abortion. She and her boyfriend, Ty, were not ready for a child even though they planned to get married in a few months, Robin said. Mary had mixed feelings about abortion. She thought it was a woman's right to choose, but she lamented the children lost. Now, her feelings jelled into one simple statement: It is wrong.

Yet, she told Otis, "If we didn't teach her before the fact, we can't force her now."

"I am just so sad about this," he replied. "I can't possibly go with her. You'll have to go. And I can't in good conscience pay for it."

"What hurts me is that Robin seems to have no real regrets. How could she not have pain?"

To Mary, the abortion was a bitterly cruel blow. She wanted children of her own blood so desperately. Now, here was a young woman who she had raised from early childhood casting off her own flesh so easily.

Five days later, Mary and Robin arrived on schedule at the abortion clinic in Houston. They waited two hours in the neat, but small waiting room. Television droning from the wall, Mary sat in the vinyl chair and watched the people as they waited. One young man sat alone reading a magazine. He looked up as a young girl came out from the office.

"Are you . . . ?" he asked.

"Yes."

"What?"

"Yes."

"Let me finish my magazine," he said, but when he noticed the irate look on her face, he set the magazine down and followed her outside.

Mary noticed what she called "clinic faces" on everyone she encountered. The Mexican couple, the two women, the attractive woman and her ordinary-looking man who kept switching the channels on the television, ending up with a cartoon.

Leaving the clinic, Mary was struck by the fact that next door stood a day care center.

Mary went home and kept the news of the day from her son and daughter. They did not know Robin had been pregnant and Robin wanted to keep it that way. Sarah moseyed in from school and announced she had been to driver's education that day.

"I can turn it on and I know where the brake and gas are, but I can't steer worth two hoots!" she said.

Otis quickly left the tension of his home and took Sarah for a driving lesson.

Robin did not hear from Ty until September. In the service in California, he wrote her that he had married someone else. He admitted he was married in Las Vegas in June, before Robin had the abortion. The wife, who was seventeen, was pregnant, too.

"I never liked him but it's hard to understand how he could be so cowardly and cruel," Mary told Otis.

In August, Mary and Otis decided to visit her parents in Knoxville and then her nieces in South Carolina. Mary especially wanted to see her namesake, Linda Mary. She had not been to Linda's house in Florence, South Carolina, since Linda's wedding a year earlier. Mary had sung at the wedding, just as she had at the

weddings of all her nieces. Linda, a Wilson High School
social studies teacher, had married a hometown boy,
Brad Watson. A salesman, he was comfortable and safe
and her mother liked him. At the time, it seemed the
right thing to do.

Leaving the men at home, Mary and Linda snuck out
for shopping at the Florence Mall and ended up at a
happy hour. Nursing a glass of white wine while sitting
across the small table from Linda, Mary recounted the
news of life in Houston. She told her niece about Sarah's
distinguished school work and Robin's new job. She
didn't tell Linda about the abortion. That was one secret
that would stay as such. Then she turned to Bob.

"He's trying to decide what to do about school," Mary
said. As she talked, the feelings she had managed to
keep below the surface for so long welled up like a
frothing volcano.

"It's so frustrating, so hard. I feel like I've done all I
could," Mary said as tears began to roll down her cheeks.
She reached inside her large handbag and pulled out
a tissue. Her voice didn't waver and she did not sob.
Tears just flowed like a trickle from a spigot.

"We have tried for so long to get Bob help," Mary
said. "A counselor told us his problems were just too
serious, that we should have him committed."

Linda was stunned. She knew that Bob could be dis-
agreeable, that he had caused problems for her auntie
Mary, but she had no idea the depth of his illness.

Mary blew her nose and continued, "I just couldn't
do it. Everybody had always given up on him, especially
women. I didn't want to give up, too." She talked on
and on. When Linda finally looked at her watch she
was surprised it was so late.

Mary McEver and Otis Coulson on their wedding day, June 24, 1967, in Knoxville, Tennessee. *(Photo courtesy of Linda Payne)*

A smiling four-year-old Bobby a few days after his adoption by Otis and Mary Coulson in August 1972. (*Photo courtesy of Peter Coulson*)

The Coulson children in February 1975: Robin, 7, Bob, 6, and Sarah, 4. (left to right) (*Photo courtesy of Peter Coulson*)

In Houston, Texas in 1976, an eight-year-old Bob Coulson poses in his Cub Scout uniform. (*Photo courtesy of Peter Coulson*)

The Coulson family in front of their former Houston home at Easter.
Robin is 9, Bob is 8, and Sarah is 5.
(*Photo courtesy of Peter Coulson*)

Four years after Bob
Coulson was confirmed
at the St. Francis
Episcopal Church
in Houston, Texas, he
was named assistant
acolyte master.   (*Photo
courtesy of Peter Coulson*)

Robin, Sarah and Bob Coulson. *(Photo courtesy of Peter Coulson)*

In June of 1992, Mary and Otis Coulson celebrated their 25th wedding anniversary. (Front row left to right) Sarah, Mary, and Otis; (Back row left to right) Robin, her husband Rick Wentworth, and Bob. *(Photo courtesy of Peter Coulson)*

The Coulsons' former Houston home just prior to the murders.
(*Photo courtesy of Peter Coulson*)

Before the murders, Coulson put a filled gasoline can in his parents' crowded garage and hid plastic bags, zip cords, and a gun in their attic. (*Photo courtesy of the Houston, Texas Police Department*)

The untouched credit cards and money in the two purses on the kitchen table convinced the police the motive for the murders was not robbery. (*Photo courtesy of the Houston, Texas Police Department*)

The telephone in Mary and Otis Coulson's bedroom melted from the intense heat of the fire. (*Photo courtesy of the Houston, Texas Police Department*)

The Coulsons' two cats were found dead in the living room. (*Photo courtesy of the Houston, Texas Police Department*)

Police located the red plastic gasoline can Coulson had thrown from the car window as he drove away from the burning house.
(*Photo courtesy of the Houston, Texas Police Department*)

The crowbar Bob Coulson took from the family garage and used to hit his sister Robin and her husband was found by the police caught in a tree limb in a ditch. (*Photo courtesy of the Houston, Texas Police Department*)

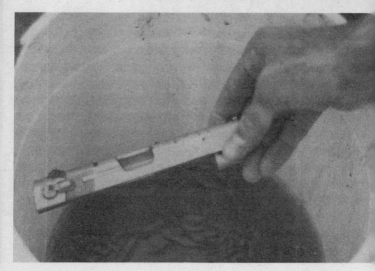

Coulson took the gun apart before throwing it out the car window. The police found the 9mm gun slide in the Yegua Creek. (*Photo courtesy of the Houston, Texas Police Department*)

Robert Coulson at the police station after being charged with capital murder in the deaths of his family. (*Photo courtesy of AP/Wide World Photos*)

Memorial stone for Otis, Mary, and Sarah Coulson.
(*Photo courtesy of Peter Coulson*)

Mary Coulson's niece, Linda Mary Payne and her husband Tim.
(*Photo courtesy of Linda Payne*)

Linda clearly did not know what to say. She uttered the only words that came to mind. She wanted to reassure her aunt, to make it all right, and she knew there were no magic words that could heal the raw hurt and frustration her aunt felt.

"I know, Auntie Mary, if anybody can help him you and Uncle O. can. He'll come around."

Mary seemed to perk up, once the venom of her emotions was out in the open.

"I don't want you to worry about this," she said. "We're going to work through this."

The early months of 1988 didn't bring newfound cheer to Mary Coulson's life. She and Otis were called to the police station after the father of Bob's girlfriend found him in her bedroom. The police let him off with a warning, but Mary was mortified.

"How could you use such bad judgment?" she asked. "We taught you good moral standards. I hope by the time you are a man you will remember them."

She told him to stay away from the girl. Within days, he was sneaking out of the house in the wee hours after everyone had gone to bed.

Coulson became increasingly distant and when he did speak to his mother it was to criticize.

"You rag on me all the time," he said. "You never let me talk."

Mary pushed him to find an apartment of his own. It was time to break the ties for good. He was nineteen. He had dropped out of school, and work was spotty. He had a new car, bought with an insurance settlement after his old car caught on fire. Some suspected he had set the car on fire himself for the insurance, but there was no proof of that.

He moved into his own apartment on the same day Mary had a hysterectomy. Mary had gone to the doctor for an ultrasound and learned she had large cysts on her ovaries. She needed immediate surgery, which was scheduled for April 15, 1988. In the eleven days until the surgery, she worried the growths were malignant.

They weren't, but the surgery solved one of the biggest mysteries of her life: why she had never been able to bear children. She had endometriosis, probably since childhood.

On the road, Friday, June 4, 1988, Mary Coulson felt the elation she had been waiting to feel for many years. She and her husband were driving their daughter, soon to be a high school senior to look at colleges. This was what all those friends from church did with their high-achieving children, and now Mary had it, too. She could barely contain her glee.

Sarah was on track to graduate in the top twenty of her class at Spring Woods Senior High. An honor student, finally. They toured Rhodes College and Oberlin. But as the summer wore on, Sarah seemed to change, to withdraw more and more from her parents. She started dating a boy Mary thought little of. "No direction," Mary told Otis.

"You'd think with this being the third one, I'd be used to this by now."

Just as Sarah was beginning her senior year, Bob came home one evening and headed straight to Sarah's room. She and Bob had always felt a closer bond than they felt with Robin, especially from Bob's standpoint. He couldn't stand Robin, even though she was his biological sister. He considered her a whale, a fat, homely girl who was not worth thinking about. He remembered how she always tried to boss him around as a child, to mother him in a way that made him uncomfortable.

Sarah was different, lithe and smart with long brown hair and a stylish albeit non-traditional flair to her dress. Coulson found her more acceptable as his sister. She did not embarrass him, either with her looks or her ways.

About forty-five minutes after Coulson and Sarah met behind her closed door, she came out and asked her mother if she could go out with him and his friends and then spend the night in his apartment. Mary answered swiftly, "No."

Coulson confronted her mother, challenging her decision. Mary held her ground.

"You should have asked us first before making a bunch of plans," she said.

He stormed from the house, angry. Mary told Sarah that was Bob's way of trying to manipulate his parents into doing what he wanted.

"Bob was trying to make decisions about what you should and should not do and then make us look like the villains for saying no," she said.

Mary wanted her youngest child to have the same independence she felt as a young girl, the same aspirations she felt as a college student, brimming with an uncharted and unlimited future. Sarah could do it, yet Mary feared she was being held back and unduly influenced by a manipulative brother and an immoral sister.

In September, Sarah was named a National Merit Semi-Finalist. Sarah took it in stride, but to Mary it was as if Sarah had won the Nobel Prize.

"Thank you Lord for preserving Sarah," she prayed that night.

But later in the fall, Mary and Otis became aware that Sarah had started drinking. After spending a Saturday night partying, Sarah came home physically and mentally exhausted. The next day, she and Mary talked it out. Sarah told her mother she felt pressured by so many things, not the least of which to achieve in school. After the talk, Mary told Otis that Sarah seemed better, things were resolved. The next week, Mary found out Sarah had started smoking.

Mary would be the first to admit that she was on the prim side, perhaps even out of touch with the modern world and its morals—or lack of them, as she would say. What bothered her most about Sarah's actions was the fact that this child was the fulfillment of her dreams and now she was sneaking around behind her parents' backs smoking, drinking and God knew what else. Whenever Sarah left the house, Mary thought, "I hope I can trust her. I want to trust her again."

As with the other two children, Mary always gave them the benefit of the doubt, looking for good in all areas.

"I wish I could understand what's going on in Sarah's head," Mary told Otis as they sat at the kitchen table one morning. "Right now, I wish she'd get up. Everything that happens these days is a struggle."

Otis responded, "On the other hand, she is doing her rebelling now, not forever, and not when she goes to college. That is a good sign."

On December 18th, Sarah was arrested for possession of alcohol in Spring Woods Park.

"I didn't have any!" she professed to her parents that night.

* * *

As the new decade dawned at the Coulson house, a wedding was in the making. Robin was to marry Rick Wentworth, a stable man with a steady job in a sporting goods store who came from a good family. His father, Wayne Wentworth, held a doctorate and worked as a chemistry professor at the University of Houston. His mother, Elise, was an attractive, vibrant housewife to whom Wayne had been married nearly forty years. They had two other sons and a daughter.

In February, the mothers accompanied Robin to see the wedding dress. Elise Wentworth demurely asked Robin if she would wear the family petticoat—the one with lace from a great-grandmother—and carry a handkerchief made from the lace of her own wedding dress.

Mary had her own handkerchief, steeped in tradition, which both she and her sister had carried.

"There's no reason you can't carry two handkerchiefs," Elise said.

"We won't hassle about the petticoat but I don't know what to do about the handkerchief," Mary later told Robin.

"I think it's tacky," Robin said to her mother's delight.

"Robin really seems to appreciate us right now," Mary told Otis that evening as they relaxed before the television set.

As always was the case in the Coulson home, good news seemed to meet bad. This time it was Sarah. She wanted to drop out of school at the end of the year. She had won a scholarship to the University of Houston but told her mother the pressure of the honors program was too much.

Mary tried to reassure her. "We care about you," she said. "Not the scholarship. It you want to dump it, we won't mind."

In the spring, Robin and Rick broke their engagement and just dated. By August, they were engaged again.

"Oh, boy!" Mary said. "Here we go again. I think this is genuine and I'm happy for them. I just hope Robin deserves him. He has certainly been faithful to her."

Robin and her mother had a grand time at Foley's Department Store, registering for china, silver, everyday dishes. So domestic. So normal.

Later that month, Bob dropped by the house. Mary was growing increasingly annoyed at his dropping by. She wanted warning, time to ready herself for his swaggering, over-confident, contemptuous ways. She especially didn't like it if he came over when no one was home. She spoke to her counselor about it, who encouraged her to tell her son to call before he came over. In times past when they had asked that of him, he became angry. He was like a child left outside the inner circle. But this time he simply said, "Okay."

He had come over to tell his parents he won first place in a driving contest at work. At twenty-two, Coulson was working for Ozarka Drinking Water, delivering bottled water to businesses. He was going to the national contest in Florida.

"We are so proud," Mary told him.

Two weeks later, Coulson came by unannounced.

"We told you to call," Mary said. "This is our house. Please respect our rights as we respect yours."

He left in a huff and didn't have any contact with his parents until his mother called him more than a week later.

On November 10th, Robin and Rick were married in a jubilant ceremony at St. Francis Episcopal Church. The huge pipe organ peeled out the majestic music of a formal ceremony. The men wore black tuxedos, the bridesmaids purple taffeta. Robin wore a calf-length gown of white, with a short veil. Two months earlier, Robin had hurt her back, picking up a child at St. Martin's Day Care Center, where she worked. Friends told her they had never seen a bride who looked so happy and in such pain at the same time.

Mary's niece Linda Mary flew in from South Carolina, the sole representative from that side of the family. Linda served as a bridesmaid and coincidentally was paired with her cousin Bob for much of the day. He escorted her out of the ceremony, just as he had walked his mother and grandmother into the church, with a stiff, toy-soldier walk, grandly strutting like a peacock.

Before the ceremony, the women gathered in a small room at the rear of the sanctuary. Everyone talked about how handsome Bob looked.

"Everything seemed focused on Bob," Linda would remember years later.

Mary was so pleased to have the occasion go off so expertly, and Robin carried both handkerchiefs.

Chapter Fifteen

Bob Coulson was many things to many people, but the one thing most everyone could agree on was that he lacked persistence. He never stuck with any type of job for any length of time. When he was twenty-two, he moved to San Antonio to work in a windshield repair business. He came home a couple of months later. He delivered water for a time, but stopped when he hurt his knee in a two-man volleyball game in the summer of 1991 and by August 1992, Bob Coulson still was not working. He told friends he had made $35,000 delivering water and was collecting almost as much on disability.

Nevertheless, shortly after he hurt his knee, he fell behind on his bills. American Express, Sears, Citibank, Kay Jewelers, his payments grew less and less frequent. By the summer of 1992, several of the businesses had charged off the accounts. They knew he would not pay. He owed $11,048 and $3,210 was past due.

His girlfriend, Jerri Moore, pressed him to find work. A successful computer saleswoman, Moore was not about to date a sloucher. Confident and attractive, Moore held a computer science degree from Illinois Benedictine in Chicago. She had moved to Houston from Chicago in July 1991. She and Coulson had met a month later. She was three years older than he and by 1992 was earning $200,000, largely from commissions. Associates called her driven and aggressive, detractors called her something else.

With Coulson not working, he became something of a house-husband for Moore. She gave him her black Toyota Celica to use after she bought an Acura. Often he would do the housework, pick up laundry and run errands because she was out of town on business usually three days a week, three weeks a month. She travelled a ten-state region from Louisiana to Montana, Arkansas to Utah. Often, she asked Coulson to use some of her frequent flier miles and come with her. He always declined.

In the latter part of 1991, Coulson borrowed $10,000 from Jerri Moore to go to Florida for a course in utility auditing. He had seen an article about this money-making business in *Entrepreneur Magazine*. This might just be the ticket to riches, he thought. She loaned him the money with the condition he repay it $500 a month, no interest. He spent a week in Florida in training, came back and told her it was a scam. No way was he doing it.

Moore was disappointed. Would he ever amount to anything? By Easter, she was fed up. They broke up, but remained friends and talked on the phone, had lunch together, sometimes were intimate. Whenever Moore went on a date with someone else, she would return to a red rose tucked in the handle of her sliding glass door. Sometimes she felt Coulson followed her or watched her. Once she returned early in the morning and found him asleep in a car in the parking lot of her condominium complex.

Coulson always seemed to have some new business prospect. He even tried to get his eighty-seven-year-old grandfather to invest in a business for him. In August 1992, he asked his father to co-sign a loan for him so he could buy a windshield repair business like the one he had worked at in San Antonio years earlier.

In the weeks before he asked his father for the loan, Coulson had become a frequent guest at the house on Westview. In July, he had spent a morning with his mother, chatting. He had talked about Jerri and their relationship.

At one point he had said to his mother, "I understand how difficult raising children—and especially me—can be."

Mary had told Otis later, "It was an extremely rewarding visit."

Coulson arrived for a family birthday party for Rick Wentworth and, except for one crude remark, was cordial.

On August 10th, Otis Coulson underwent surgery for his arthritic knees. He awoke to the good news that his daughter Robin was pregnant.

"April will be the target date, Grandpa," Mary said, smiling. She was happy for her daughter, but most relieved that her husband had come through the surgery well. With the difference in their ages, she worried he was on the downhill side of life. She didn't know how to live without him.

Coulson stayed with his mother during the day of the surgery and Robin spent the night with her.

"I'm not too comfortable staying alone," she said. Robin happily agreed to stay with her mother.

Two days after the surgery, Coulson started pushing his father about a decision on the loan.

"You have to tell Bob to back off," Mary told Otis.

"I know. I know," he said. He had thought through the request and would not loan Bob the money outright but would co-sign if Bob would give him personal financial information. He didn't want to liquidate any of his stocks or bonds.

The next day, Coulson passed the morning with Otis in the hospital.

Mary hoped it was at least partly because he wanted to be with Otis and not because he wanted money. She was feeling pushed by Bob about the money and still had hard feelings about his selfishness and role playing. She hoped it wouldn't turn into a hassle.

Coulson went back to the owner to tell him financing was all set. He was ready to do business. Unfortunately, someone else had come up with the cash first and the owner had already sold it.

Sometime later, Jason Althaus heard Coulson say, "My parents have screwed me for the last time. I'm going to kill them."

Burglaries occurred from time to time in the Spring Woods subdivision, but fear was uncommon among residents. The Tuckers had been robbed and the Bodenhamers, too. Mary and Otis Coulson had been lucky. No big-city crime had come knocking at their door.

But sometime in 1991, they installed a sophisticated burglar alarm, which dialed a telephone number to dispatch a security guard to investigate the trouble. They didn't broadcast the fact they installed the system, and Otis' brother Peter assumed it was because Sarah had had some strange experiences with boyfriends. One of them had stalked her after she had broken up with him. He had left her alone only after Bob Coulson had confronted him at the front door of the house one night.

Mary met weekly with a religion study group at her church. She was the mentor for the group, which often shared prayers for each other and for their friends and loved ones. In the fall of 1992, Mary regularly asked for special prayers for troubles she was having with her family. She would not be specific about her problems, but her intensity showed through. One member knew that Mary had grown increasingly uneasy about her son.

"He haunted her," the member said. "He was growing increasingly angry; she had a feeling something was very wrong with him. He wasn't pleased with life, nothing was enough. He wanted more of life and people and times."

One of the family's favorite traditions was their Friday night dinners. But in 1992, they started going out to eat rather than eating Mary's fine cooking at home. Invariably Coulson and Robin would wind up in a fight, often escalating to fury. If they were in public, Coulson would behave.

"I am uncomfortable about Bob's anger," Mary confided to a friend. "I never know what he's thinking but I know he's thinking."

One night in October, Mary Coulson was awakened by her dogs barking wildly outside her sliding glass door. Her husband, who wore hearing aides in both ears during the day, rested quietly by her side. Mary leaped from bed and silently crept into the bathroom in her master bedroom suite so she could look out the window and onto the patio.

She carefully raised her head to see. Standing at the door was a dark figure, a man. He was toying with the door handle, perhaps trying to pick the lock. Mary made a sound and when the man turned to run off, she thought she could tell who it was. It was Bob.

The next day, the Coulsons installed floodlights in their backyard.

Burdened, sorrowful, angry, the hot emotions flowed freely from Mary Coulson when her daughter Sarah told her she was pregnant. Sarah was unmarried and had no serious boyfriend. Mary and Otis were shattered. This was the child in whom their dreams of success resided. Mary didn't tell anyone the news for a long time, not Bob or Robin, and she never told her parents. She wanted to spare them the shock. But perhaps more importantly, she wanted to spare Sarah their disappointment.

The baby's father was not the boy she'd been dating regularly, but someone with whom she had had a brief fling. Mary considered that fact the cruelest one of all.

But as she had done all her life, Mary poured out unconditional love for her daughter and invited her to return home. Sarah continued to live in her apartment with her roommate Dawn Ceyba until just before the baby was born. One night about a week before Sarah's baby was due, she and her mother spent a quiet evening at home.

Mary rubbed Sarah's back to relax her. As Mary brushed Sarah's long brown hair, they talked about the baby, which would be given up for adoption through an Episcopal agency.

"I am worried about the delivery, Mother," Sarah confided.

"I know my darling. I know."

It was tough riding the emotional rollercoaster of her own feelings and those of her daughters, Robin, who was bearing her husband's child and Sarah, who would give her baby to a couple she knew not. On October 27, 1992, the baby Mary called her first and not her first grandchild was born. Sarah delivered a 6-pound, 14-ounce boy by caesarean section. The operation was done as an emergency because Sarah had a herpes lesion. Sarah named him Eric.

Two days later, a Thursday, Mary witnessed Sarah signing the adoption papers. She called it the "hardest day of her life."

That night, Mary wrote in her journal, "The baby—Eric—is precious and lovable and dear and we all grieve for his loss. Lord, bless this one, my strong child and her darling son who is no longer going to be a Coulson. We will miss you Eric and you will always be in our hearts."

On Friday, they said goodbye.

"Now we begin the healing process," Mary said when they got home from the hospital. "Sarah you will be okay."

On Sunday, All Saints Day, Sarah spent the afternoon crying for her child. On Wednesday, six-day-old Eric went to a wealthy family in Houston. The mother was a lawyer.

In the second week of November 1992, tension ruled the Coulsons' household. Otis felt irritable. Mary studied her husband and thought he looked old. Sarah wept frequently. Robin bounced from happy to sad. No one saw Bob.

Mary had already started her Christmas shopping, mainly those hard-to-buy presents for her sister's family in South Carolina. She chose plaid flannel shirts for the men and Christmas ornaments for her grandniece and grandnephews.

The days moved ahead as the rhythm of life regained its normal beat. They went to church on Sunday and, afterward, Mary practiced with the handbell group at her friend Maggi's church. The next weekend she and Maggi would go to a handbell festival in Spring, Texas.

Later Sunday evening, Rick and Robin took Mary to see the movie *Sister Act*. Just what she needed, some laughs. "Delightful and entertaining," was how she described it later. Tuesday, Mary and Otis celebrated Rick and Robin's second anniversary with a special breakfast. How good their lives looked right then, a happy marriage for Robin and a grandchild on the way, one that was wanted and cherished. The baby would sleep in the cradle Dicko made so many years before. Tradition. Family. It was all Mary ever wanted.

After breakfast, Mary drove to the church to plan a retirees luncheon with one of the ministers. More Christmas shopping next. Her list was long. She bought for every member of the family, close and extended.

Wednesday Robin had a sonogram and announced to her happy parents that her baby was a girl. She would be called Hayden Elise Wentworth, Hayden for Mary—it was her middle name, one she shared with her beloved great-uncle who was an opera singer—and Elise for Rick's mother. Mary had started a journal for the baby on August 10th, the same day Robin and Rick revealed her existence. In it, she told the baby about Otis' surgery that day, adding, "We love you already!" Mary had completed a cross-stitched quilt for the baby, who she laughingly called "Wee Whimsical Wentworth." Rick didn't think that was too funny. On the day of the sonogram, Rick and Robin bought Hayden a pink puffalump and placed it carefully in her crib. The nursery was already ready for the daughter they expected to see sometime in April.

On Friday, Otis went as usual to Memorial Assistance Ministries, a co-op run by a number of Houston churches for needy families. He volunteered many hours there each week. Otis had little trouble occupying himself in retirement. Once he feared he would be bored. But busyness seemed to find him easily. He worked around the house and kept track of his investments.

Friday night, the family would gather at the house for their regular family-night supper. Robin and Rick were almost always there on Fridays, and Sarah was often home, too. Bob came every now and then. Waiting for her children to arrive, Mary took out her journal and started writing, carefully topping it with the date, November 13, 1992. She would never finish the entry.

PART III:
The Trial

Chapter Sixteen

Case No. 9400472, the State of Texas versus Robert O. Coulson came to trial on May 31, 1994, one and a half years after Mary and Otis Coulson, Sarah Coulson, Rick and Robin Wentworth and their unborn daughter were bound, gagged and set on fire in the Coulson's Houston home. Prosecutor Chuck Rosenthal elected to try Bob Coulson only on the deaths of his biological sister, Robin and her husband. His star witness, Jared Althaus, Coulson's former roommate, would testify that Coulson told him he smothered his mother with a pillow. Detectives never found a pillow in the room, a discrepancy. With the Wentworths, the evidence was clear. Coulson told Jared he beat them with a crowbar, which police recovered.

The trial would pit Chuck Rosenthal against Jim Skelton, two lawyers with little good to say about the other. The differences were as stark as the clothes they wore to speak at a convention. Rosenthal showed up in a business suit; Skelton wore blue jeans, a tuxedo jacket and shirt and different colored cowboy boots.

A former assistant district attorney, Skelton was as apt to be found riding a motorcycle to Oregon as defending a client in a Houston courtroom. He kept his silver hair long and swept under at the back. Known for his scholarly opening and closing arguments, he often quoted the Bible and Socrates or spouted history lessons. Rosenthal was more folksy, with a smooth tongue, particularly when he felt impassioned about something. He was a lumbering man, tall with thick silver hair. He looked like the kind of Texan who would be comfortable in cowboy boots, but, if he was, he never wore them to court. He fell into law because he didn't want to study business and went to the D.A.'s office in Harris County with the intention of getting some trial experience and moving on to a high-paying law career. That was in 1976; he never left.

Every year, Texas executes more men than any state, and Harris County, where Houston is located, leads the state in the number of men on Death Row. District Attorney Johnny Holmes believes if a law is on the books, it ought to be enforced. The death penalty is the law of the land. By itself, Harris County hands out more death sentences than some states.

The judge would be Donald K. Shipley. Before he was elected to a judgeship, he often could be seen between cases making balloon animals in the basement commissary. Shipley was not a favorite of the media. He placed a gag order on the lawyers in the Coulson case after a story quoting unnamed sources said a secret diary named Bob Coulson as the father of Sarah's baby. The report set off a rush of commotion, from family members who wondered if it could be true, to the baby's adoptive parents, who wanted to know for sure. DNA tests proved it false. There was no secret diary. Shipley also banned cameras from the courtroom.

Jury selection took twenty-seven days. A total of one hundred fifteen people were excused before twelve jurors and an alternate were seated. The balance would be five men, seven women. The alternate was a woman. Lawyers agonize over jury selection. They read jurors' questionnaires, watch body language, ask lots of questions prospective jurors have never even thought about before and then end up with a bunch of people they don't really know. It's a crap shoot.

Chuck Rosenthal rarely gave opening statements, but in the Coulson case he felt he had to. Some threads needed tying together. He rose and walked toward the panel.

"Some of the first firemen inside the door, fighting through the smoke and the heat in that inferno that was the house, found a body and then another, another, another and another. Five bodies inside that house. You're going to find that the firemen found and then later police investigations show that those people had been tied up, every one of those people had been suffocated with a plastic bag."

Rosenthal told them almost immediately that Coulson did it "for money purely out of greed."

"He planned this event for months and months. Several days prior to the killing he took all the equipment he would need to the house and stored it in the house so it would be there and available for him when he went there on Friday afternoon and killed those folks. He knew they would be there. Every Friday afternoon the family met for a family dinner. You're going to find they didn't have one enemy in the world, none of them did, other than that man right there.''

He pointed to Coulson, sitting demurely in an oxford cloth shirt and tie and trousers. He looked like an Ivy League prepster, complete with wire-rimmed glasses. No one had seen Bob Coulson wear glasses since the ninth grade. He was too vain for that.

Coulson's lawyer Jim Skelton told the jury, ''The evidence in this case is going to indicate throughout the involvement of Jared Althaus.'' Althaus is the one, Skelton pointed out, who worked a deal for a twenty-year sentence for his involvement in the murders, not Coulson who faced the death penalty.

Rosenthal set up his case by calling the people who were first on the scene, Bill Lobins, the fireman who found Robin Wentworth, pregnant, bound by her wrists, ankles and knees, dead just feet from the one man who loved her completely, her husband Rick.

Lobins said when he arrived at the Coulson home he saw flames and a lot of smoke pouring from the residence.

''Were you to fight the fire or were you searching for people?'' Rosenthal asked.

''Our primary concern is to save lives and search for people.''

He explained that he and his men crawled through the house.

''I found a woman's feet; and I knew it was a woman

immediately because I saw a white brassiere, and she was lying on her side."

"Do you know which side she was lying on?"

"She was lying on her right side."

"Okay."

"She was in a peculiar position."

"Well, how so?"

"It was like her feet were together and her arms were together in front of her like this. Then when I looked closer, they were tied. I grabbed her, and then I realized she was dead."

One by one, they found the rest of the bodies, Lobins said. And one by one, the men who saw the remains of the lives of the Coulson family came to court to tell the story. Bill Sammons, the chief investigator with the Houston Fire Department, was asked if there was anything unusual about the conditions of the individuals inside the house.

"Their hands and feet were taped," he said. "They had plastic bags over their heads."

"Have you seen that kind of situation before?"

"I've seen people tied up. I've never seen the plastic bag over the head before."

"As an arson investigator or someone skilled in that craft, did you see anything characteristic of where an accelerant—for instance, like gasoline—had been thrown inside there?"

He had. A pattern remained on the floor, all over the room.

It was slopped on the beds, on the bodies. Sammons said some victims were bound with plastic tie wraps, which are used to wrap wire and sometimes as handcuffs.

On the first day of the trial, Rosenthal hit the attentive

jury with the horrible and the gruesome. Dozens of photographs taken by the crime scene unit were introduced as evidence and shown to the jury. The plastic bag oozing from Robin's face. The bindings. The melted telephone. The dead cats.

An assistant medical examiner, Tommy J. Brown, revealed the results of the autopsies. "Robin Wentworth, 25, 66 inches in length, 201 pounds in weight. She was severely burned over her body, estimated at 95 percent total body surface burns. She had in place a plastic—white plastic bag over her head that was burned and also some duct tape around her mouth and her nose. There was a one-inch imprint around the neck also from the duct tape at the base of the white plastic bag. Her hands were tied around the wrist, and her hands were in front of her with partially burned duct tape around the wrist and also some other thick plastic that was described as nonspecific and not otherwise specified. She had second-degree—second- and third-degree of the face, greater than two-thirds of the face. The eyes were cooked, her left ear and nose were cooked. Her upper lip was also severely burned. She had second- and third-degree burns of the neck. She had an imprint around the neck. She had second- and third-degree burns of the abdomen, both legs. Also her upper extremities, her arms and her back. She had partially burned duct tape around her right, lower leg that was burned into. Ninety-five percent of her body had second- or third-degree burns."

Brown explained the difference between burns. Third-degree means the burn goes entirely through the skin, and cannot be regenerated, second-degree the skin can be regenerated and first-degree is sunburn.

Robin was six months pregnant. The baby was a girl. The autopsy showed she, like all the other members of her family, were dead when she was set on fire.

Brown continued detailing the autopsies for the jury.

"Richard Robert Wentworth, 27, 73 inches in length, 290 pounds, white male, his head was covered with a plastic bag. He had gray duct tape over his mouth and to the back of his neck that was two inches in width. His legs were tied and there was melted duct tape around them, and he had thick plastic ties around both ankles. Both his hands were tied at the back with three thick plastic ties. There were second- and third-degree burns of the upper face, back of the head, back of the neck, posterior arms and forearms, the back of the thighs, the lower legs. The back was also severely burned. His left ear was charred. The right ear had third-degree burns. There was a large bruise along the back of the left shoulder that was not described in the autopsy report. Approximately 75 percent total body surface burned, second- and third-degree burns.

"Mary Coulson, 54, 63 inches in height, 234 pounds, melted plastic bag over her head as well as duct tape on her nose and mouth, second- and third-degree burns on 100 percent of her body. Her upper extremities were not tied behind her. They were put up in front of her rather than being bound together.

"Otis Coulson, 66, 5'8", 135 pounds, white male with a melted white plastic bag, was reinforced by duct tape around the neck, hands tied at the back, 95 percent total body surface area second- and third-degree burns.

"Sarah Coulson, 21-year-old white female, 66 inches length, 130 pounds. She had 70 percent total body surface area burned, second- and third-degrees. She had melted duct tape around her left wrist that had burned into it. She also had a left large, gray leg brace on her left lower extremity. She had a partially burned plastic bag with melted duct tape around her head. Her eyes were cooked. She had second- and third-degree burns of her head. Second- and third-degree over the entire anterior torso and upper and lower extremities, comprising 70 percent of total body surface area.''

After the harrowing, Rosenthal moved to the sorrowful. He called Wayne Wentworth, Rick's father, who testified about his four children, now missing the youngest, and his wife of forty years.

As Rosenthal wove the story of a selfish, young man, friends and family members testified to the goodness of the family. Peter Coulson was asked if the Coulsons had enemies who would want to see them die.

''No, indeed. No, indeed,'' he said.

''Have you ever known a gentler person than your brother Otis?

''No. I believe my brother was the most gentle man I have ever known in my life.''

Peter told the jury Bob Coulson visited him in San Marcos on the Wednesday before the murders on Friday. They talked about Coulson's knee injury. Peter couldn't remember whether Coulson asked him if he planned to go to Houston for the weekend. But he knew then in his heart that Coulson had come to visit to see if he would be there that day. Peter felt sure if he had, he would have been killed, too. He sometimes wondered how he could have been so naive about Bob in the beginning. It just never crossed his mind.

On cross-examination from Coulson's lawyers, Peter

said he thought the feuding between Robin and Bob was simply sibling rivalry, nothing more.

The lawyer asked, "Who would be the one more or less running the family? In this family, who would wear the pants, would you say?"

"Well, Otis and Mary—certainly it was a give-and-take relationship, but I would say that Mary was the more dominant of the two."

The defense tried to chip away at the state's witnesses, hammering home the point that all the Coulsons except possibly Sarah were strong, strapping people, able to defend themselves. Yet Bob Coulson suffered no bruises, no singed hair, no burns.

"None," said Detective Dale Achetee, the first policeman on the scene that night, when asked if he saw anything out of the ordinary about Coulson's appearance. Later he would say of Coulson's lack of wounds, "Bob Coulson is one lucky bastard."

Coulson's onetime girlfriend, Jerri Moore, testifying for the prosecution, told the court that she met him in a country and western bar called The Rose. He asked her to dance. She remembered the date: August 8, 1991. She had been in Houston a month, after relocating there for her work. She saw his parents from time to time, at Thanksgiving dinner and Christmas before she and Bob flew to Chicago.

"They came to my condo when I bought the condo, took them for a ride when I got the new car. So we— it was not all that often."

"Did there seem to be any enmity or any problems between Mary Coulson and the defendant?"

"Not—not to my knowledge."

"Was she cordial to you as to someone who was dating her son?"

"Yes. Very much so."

"And basically would talk to you about what kinds of things?"

"Little Bob stories, when he was growing up or those types of things."

"Can you describe what his sense of humor is and how he would react to you and other people?"

"Well, one of the things that Bob and I had a bit of contention with is that he would put me down, I guess, in front of others in general, and that bothered me."

"Was he uniformly that way or would he react differently around other folks?"

"He would say it to me directly, and he would—it would probably get a little more out of hand when he was around other people."

"Well, specifically, when he was around his parents or around your parents, was he as caustic in his comments to you?"

"Around his parents, no. Around my parents, yes."

"Did you ever have the occasion to see Jared Althaus and Bob Coulson together?"

"Yes."

"Did you see anything that showed you which of the two was a leader or a follower or manifested a stronger personality?"

"I think it was just evident by their personalities that Bob was the stronger personality of the two."

Rosenthal asked Jerri Moore if she was out of town the weekend before the Coulsons died. She returned on the Monday before the murders. Coulson picked her up at the airport in her Acura and told her that he and Jared were planning a trip to the farm for the weekend. She became enraged.

"I traveled a lot and had offered to take him with me out of town on several occasions, and he always said that he didn't want to go out of town, so I was rather upset that he would decide to go out of town with Jared when he never—over the past year and a half—wouldn't go out of town with me."

Coulson surprised Jerri at her office the night before his parents were murdered. He came in around seven, dressed in jeans, boots, button-down, starched shirt and he politely handed her a rose.

"Did Mr. Coulson, either that evening or any evening before that, give you any indication that led you to believe that he had followed you?"

"Yes, he did," Moore replied, remembering a couple of times. Once, he knew a man she was dating was from the North. Another time, he saw a name on her desk and knew it was a fellow she had gone out with.

"Did you ask him about those things?"

"Yes, I did."

"And what would he tell you?"

"He would say, 'I'm Bob, and I know everything.'"

Moore had a date with someone else on the Thursday Coulson visited her in her office. He walked her to her Acura. Her Celica, which he was driving, was parked nearby. They made plans to have lunch the next day after she made a sales presentation. As planned, she called Coulson after her meeting, but couldn't reach him so she went back to work. He phoned at 1:00 P.M. She'd already made other plans with coworkers to go to lunch.

Jerri Moore said she learned of the murders Saturday

night when a police sergeant called her. She raced down to the police department, saw Coulson in the hall but couldn't speak with him. She left to hire an attorney for him but by the time they returned, he had gone. She drove to his apartment, where Jared Althaus let her in. He seemed very upset, shaken.

"I said, 'What happened?' "

"He said, 'I don't know. I don't know.' "

Coulson's eyes looked red but he was composed. They walked into his bedroom to talk. He hugged her a few times.

'What happened?" she asked.

"Jared and I went out of town that weekend, and I just found out about it today," he answered.

He told her about the gas receipt.

She stayed between thirty and forty-five minutes. Moore told the jury she was "scared to death of whoever did this" and didn't go back to her apartment for two weeks. She stayed with a friend.

After Coulson's arrest, Moore was asked to identify some items. The police showed her a picture of a navy blue Champion sweatshirt. It was like the one her parents had given him for Christmas. Also among the pictures was one of a baseball cap Coulson had borrowed from her three months earlier. He had worn the clothes her mother bought for him to kill his family.

"You testified earlier that after the Saturday following the murders, when you had seen Mr. Coulson, that you were afraid and you wouldn't go back to your condominium," Rosenthal said.

"Right."

"Are you still afraid?"

"Yes, I am."

"Of who?"

"Bob."

As the second day drew to an end, Moore's answer lingered in the air like the smell from a sewage plant.

Chapter Seventeen

Trial witnesses could not stay in the courtroom during testimony, so Linda Payne and other prosecution witnesses stayed in a room next door. It looked much like a doctor's waiting room, decorated with couches and tables. A television, magazines and a phone were provided to help witnesses pass the time. A victim's advocate sat at a desk inside to comfort witnesses and to make sure no one other than the prosecution's witnesses came inside. They had a special buzzer to unlock the door. Most of the other witnesses spent short intervals in the room, waiting to be called to testify, then they'd go home.

Linda Payne spent every minute of the trial there. While her brother and sister were there, they would come out during breaks and tell her what was going on, other times some of the prosecution team would fill her in. Most of the time, she'd write end-of-the-year letters to her teacher cadets, a tradition she had started years before as a way to encourage them. As she was coming out of the room one afternoon, Bob Coulson was leaving the courtroom, escorted by the bailiffs. She stopped to let the entourage pass. A bailiff opened the door to the holding cell and Linda could see inside. Coulson had placed newspapers on the floor so his feet wouldn't have to touch the floor when he changed back into his orange prison jumpsuit.

First order of business on the third trial day was the defense's stab at cracking Jerri Moore's portrait as a former girlfriend in fear of a monster. Jim Skelton prodded her into describing herself as aggressive, a top performer in a viciously competitive business, computer sales. He asked how long she had dated Coulson when she gave him a key to her apartment. About a month, she replied, and he echoed her answer for emphasis.

"About a month," he said, strongly as if making a moral judgment. He wanted the jury to see that Bob Coulson had no reason to murder his parents for money when he could have had a rich and attractive wife.

"You were—to understate it—rather successful for a twenty-seven-year-old young lady, were you not?" the lawyer asked.

"Yes, I was."

"And it was rather obvious—was it not?—that you were successful in talking to Bob? He knew this, didn't he?"

"Bob knew this, yes."

"Would he have a chance, if he'd chosen to, to marry you? Would that have been a possibility?"

"During what time?"

"During the period of time up until you broke up with him."

"Easter?"

"Yes, ma'am."

"Yes. It would have been a possibility."

Later, the lawyer asked Moore, "At your request, we got the bailiff to put Bob in a room off in the back where you and me and Bob were all in the room together. Isn't that correct?"

"That's correct."

"Now, the man that you've testified to that you've been fearful of, you spent how long with Bob in that room back there?"

"I don't know. Thirty minutes, maybe. You were there."

"Embraced him how many times during that period of time?"

"I gave him a hug twice."

"As a matter of fact, when this gentleman over here, the bailiff, came to pick him up, you embraced him in his presence. Is that correct?"

"That was the second time."

"Right."

"And as a matter of fact, even at breaks here today, you've been back talking to Bob just a while ago?"

"Right."

"Isn't that correct?"

"Yes."

"And you don't think the conduct that you've exhibited by what you've just described is inconsistent with the idea that you're fearful of Bob?"

"I think it depends on how you define fearful."

"Right."

"I mean, do I think he's going to jump up and do anything with a bailiff standing there? Absolutely not."

Skelton tried to make Moore admit that she only made negative comments about Coulson because she was afraid her relationship with him would hurt her business. She stood her ground, saying there was nothing inconsistent in her actions.

On redirect, Rosenthal asked, "You've carried on a relationship with him since then. Why?"

"Well, part of the reason was because—it started out because I thought that he was fairly vulnerable in jail, and he led me to believe through a variety of conversations that he could not continue on without these phone calls. And he had already—based upon what he had said at the jail that day, I was thinking, 'God, if I had gone to lunch that day.' And now I'm thinking, 'What if he commits suicide in jail because I don't talk to him?' So I wasn't going to have that hanging over my head."

"Is there any other reason why you accepted calls and talked to him?"

"Then, like I said before, I was scared of him, and I was kind of afraid, actually. I kind of know what some of the evidence is. I've been in contact with a variety of people, and I don't—I don't know what the outcome of this trial will be, and I certainly don't want to tick him off."

The courtroom burst into laughter.

Nervous and knowing at any minute she might cry, Linda Payne trudged to the witness stand and sat down.

Rosenthal asked her about the woman she called "Auntie Mary."

"She was single until later in her life," Linda began, "so she was with my family a lot for family vacations and holidays. We had always been close growing up, so she took on a real active role after my mama had died to help try and take care of us."

Rosenthal asked her about a phone call she received from Bob Coulson late Sunday night after the murders.

"It was about my plans to come out for the memorial service, it was about being involved in the will, it was about the process that we would have to go through to settle the will, it was about securing permission to get into the house because he felt like the house was unsecured and he needed my permission before he could remove items. And it was where we would be staying and about what I would need to do as soon as I got out here in order for him to be able to get the will in motion and settled, and he wanted to do it as quickly as possible so I could get back home."

"Ms. Payne, was there a lot of emotion in his voice?"

"There was—there was an edge to his voice," she said. "It wasn't emotional, it was very short, and it was very clipped. And then as far as when we talked about arrangements—I was bringing up what had happened to his family—there was no emotion in his voice as we talked about his family."

"Did he make any inquiries of when it was that you were appointed or named as executrix?"

"Yes, he did. In fact, he seemed to be very surprised that I was at all involved. He had found out that I was coming to Texas, and he wasn't sure why. And he had been told that it was not only to come to the memorial service but because I'm executrix. He wanted to know when I had been contacted by my aunt for that and how I had gotten involved and if I had a copy of the will and what I knew about the probate court system. And that he had also been told that I would have to sign before he could get in the house, and he needed me to come sign for that.''

Linda recounted all her conversations with Coulson before and after the funeral. Then defense attorney Robert Pelton rose to cross-examine her.

"I know this is a very unpleasant position that you're in right now, and I understand that, and I understand you're a little bit nervous about being up here or a great deal nervous about being up here."

"I don't usually testify in murder cases," Linda said.

"I understand that. And I hope you understand that probably everybody in here is a little bit nervous about this whole situation because there's people in the audience, there's people—prosecutors, lawyers, newspaper people, people writing books about this case. I'm sure we're all a little bit nervous. I'm sure maybe some of the jurors are nervous about being here today. I don't mind telling you I'm nervous about being here. So I hope you understand some of the things that I'm going to talk to you about. And I know they're very sensitive things, and I'm not trying to cause you any more anguish or any more grief than you already have, because I know that you were very close to your family and especially close to Mary Coulson. I understand that. If you would, go back—this tragedy occurred on Friday the 13th. November 13th, 1992. And would you tell me again when was the first time that you heard anything about this horrible tragedy that happened?"

"Early Saturday morning."

Pelton pressed Linda Payne on details of the Coulsons' wills, trying to make it look like she was the greedy lady cousin from South Carolina that no one had ever heard of.

"This is a copy of Mary Coulson's will. If you would, take just a minute, ma'am, and read this part right here. Please read it out loud.

"Can I just give her a copy?" he asked the judge who agreed.

"If you would, just read it out loud," Pelton continued.

"In the event my husband and my children should predecease me and fail to leave issue, I give all the rest, residue and remainder of my property to my nieces and nephews, in equal shares, per stipends."

"Now those people that you've just read off out of this will, would you tell the jury who those folks are, please?"

"They're my brothers and my sisters."

"Okay."

"Has anyone told you or do you know from your own personal knowledge whether or not any of those folks have made a claim on this estate?"

"None of these people have."

"So as far as you know, the way it stands now, if Bob is convicted of killing his family, he's not going to get any of this money?"

"Well, no. What I understand is you have to go through a different process to show that he's not supposed to get that money. That that's not a given. There's another process to go through."

"Would you tell the jury whether or not you're getting paid a fee for being the executrix of this will?"

"I've been told that after the will is settled, I will get a certain percentage payment for the executrix fee."

"And would you tell this jury, please, how much of a percentage of this estate are you going to get for being the executrix of this will?"

"I don't know."

"But you at least—do you know that you're going to get some money out of this estate for doing all these things that you've had to do for taking—helping prepare these inventories and for coming down here and for meeting with the lawyers and this sort of thing?"

"Do you understand that there's no amount of money in the world that could pay me for what I've been through personally and professionally?" Linda asked pointedly.

"Yes, ma'am. I understand that."

"I don't know what the set fee is, and whatever is given to me for a set fee, I hope can be used for my grandparents."

"I understand. I understand that. And that's why it's unpleasant for me to have to ask you this, Ms. Payne, but it's something that I have to ask you. Now, do you know whether or not the executor of Otis' will is going to get paid a fee for doing that?"

"Yes."

Mike Scott, twenty-six, started off the fourth day's testimony. In 1992, he was working for a civil engineering firm as a computer technician. Coulson and Scott had been friends since their first year of high school. They both played the trumpet in the band. Also in the band were Jared Althaus, who was a year younger, and Scott Smith. After high school, Scott attended Stephen F. Austin State University in Nacogdoches, Texas, while Coulson went to Southwest Texas in San Marcos.

"Did there come a time when you, Jared Althaus and Bob Coulson decided to rent an apartment together?"

"Yes, we did."

"Do you remember, to the best of your knowledge, when the three of you leased an apartment together?"

"Sometime in the spring of '92."

"How did y'all decide to live together?"

"Well, I was living with my mother at the time, and Jared had his own apartment. I was looking to get out of my parents' house, so I asked Jared if he wanted to get a room together. At the same time, Bob was living in an apartment that he had been in for quite some time paying month to month, and they were raising the rent; and he was tired of paying that."

They split the $825 monthly rent three ways. Coulson used his disability payments.

"What kind of things did the three of you do?"

"Happy hours, you know, dance places and maybe some bowling. We were in a league."

"During that two-month period, did your relationship with the defendant and Jared Althaus deteriorate?"

"Yes, it did."

Scott started feeling like the outsider as Althaus took on much of Coulson's abrasive personality, rather than his usual do-anything-for-you demeanor. They liked to play a game called "One Up" or "Dozens." Players try to come up with the last word, the best, the put down, to make the others look stupid.

Scott decided to housesit for a friend to get out of the increasingly unpleasant atmosphere in the apartment, although he continued to split the rent, just in case he needed to move back in.

Jeannine Barr, the assistant district attorney, asked Scott if Coulson had made any unusual comments about his family. He remembered Coulson saying, "Goddamn, my parents are spending my inheritance."

"Now, did you also hear him make any comments about the family being on their way to Europe and the plane crashing or something to that effect?"

"Yes, I did."

Scott said Bob said it in jest, it was flip.

He called his sister fat and lazy and his mother obese.

"What about any derogatory comments about Otis Coulson?"

"There was an occasional comment that, you know, that his dad just—his dad, being disabled, wasn't really—you know, I don't recall anything specific about his dad."

"Can you think of any specific examples of fact situations where Bob and Jared would interact that showed that Bob had the stronger personality?"

"If one went upstairs, the other one would follow, if one went downstairs, the other would follow. If one would suggest going to eat—if Bob would suggest going to eat here, Jared would go—Bob controlled basically what they did together."

"Like out on a date or something?"

"At clubs and also dealing with his girlfriends. 'Go talk to that girl. Tell her this.' Jared would just do it."

"Was he more or less like Bob's puppet?"

"Yeah."

* * *

Barr called Christine Allen Donlin, a property manager, who remembered Bob Coulson coming to her office three days before the murders to look at a $1,000-a-month penthouse apartment.

Chapter Eighteen

After the weekend break, testimony resumed Monday with Scott Smith, Coulson's friend.

"I think you were with Bob when he hurt his leg," Robert Pelton asked on cross-examination.

"That's correct."

"And y'all were playing volleyball, weren't you?"

"We were playing volleyball."

"He wasn't at work when he hurt his leg, was he?"

"Right."

"And you know that after he hurt his leg, he had to have surgery done?"

"Yes."

"If you remember or know, would you tell the ladies and gentlemen of the jury what kind of surgery he had done?"

"It was a knee reconstruction." Smith explained.

"You know that Bob's under a lot of stress right now.

You can tell by looking at him because—can't you—because you've known him?"

"That's my observation."

"And you've known him, and know how he acts under stress, don't you?"

"Yes."

"And I think you told—told me earlier that you've never seen Bob cry, have you?" Pelton pressed.

"No."

"Because Bob's the kind of guy that keeps things inside himself?"

"Yes."

"During those fifteen years, sixteen years that you knew Bob Coulson, the time that you've known him, you've met some of his relatives, haven't you?"

"Yes."

"And you've met his cousin—his uncle Peter, I think, from San Marcos?"

"Yes."

"And you've met, of course, his other two sisters and his mom and dad?"

"Yes."

"You've never met a cousin of his named Linda Payne, though, did you?"

"Not until this trial."

"All right. And all those years that you knew Bob and all those times that you went to their house, you never met this cousin from South Carolina, did you?"

"No, I didn't."

Linda Payne arrived at the courthouse on the trial's sixth day and as usual buzzed to get into the witness

room. The victim advocate seemed slightly edgy, Linda
thought. Then she saw why. Jared Althaus, the man who
helped her cousin kill her aunt, was standing inside
talking with the prosecutor. Althaus quickly walked over
to Linda and put his arm around her back.

"I'm so sorry, I'm so sorry," he said.

Linda did not know what to say. She fumbled for
words. As with most Southern women, she was hard-
pressed to confront him. Matters of courtesy and respect
take front stage in the rearing of Southern children and
it was a lesson Linda had learned well. You don't make
a scene. Yet, here was the guy who allowed this to happen
to her aunt, to her.

Finally, she said, "My family appreciates what you are
trying to do now. We know you are helping our family."

She turned on her heels and went into the bathroom,
where she remained for long time.

Althaus was the kind of kid most everybody has in at
least one class. He's just there. No apparent flair for
anything. He had been diagnosed with attention deficit
disorder as a child, making school an ordeal. Just before
he moved in with Bob Coulson, his parents had kicked
him out of the house. He didn't like to talk about it,
but his relationship with his parents had been strained
for years.

After Althaus was sworn in, Prosecutor Rosenthal
came straight to the point.

"Was there a plan between you and the defendant
to kill his parents, Mary and Otis Coulson?"

"Yes."

"And about when did that plan begin? About how
long before their deaths did it begin?"

"Approximately three to four months."

"Was it your plan or was it—who initiated the plan?"

"Mr. Coulson did."

"How did he first approach the idea to you, if you recall?"

"He first approached it to me when we were watching *Cops*, one of those shows on TV, and he mentioned that he wanted to kill his parents. And at first, I just shrugged it off as he was joking, but he constantly brought it up, almost on a daily basis."

Althaus, looking earnest, told the jury that Coulson had wanted him to take part in the actual killings, but he had refused.

"I was to take him to the house and pick him up and support him with an alibi."

They began collecting the items needed to kill the family three months before the murders actually took place, Althaus testified. They bought duct tape, the cable ties and the stun gun. Coulson liked the idea of the stun gun because he wanted to immobilize his family members. They shopped around for just the right model. They ended up at a firearms place off Highway 6, between 59 and I-10. The same day he purchased zip ties and duct tape. Later he got the trash compactor bags.

"I came home one day from work," Althaus said. "and Bob was all excited and happy and said he had a surprise for me. And he pulled out trash compactor bags, and he said that he went to the store and pulled each one out of the bag and he tried it for toughness to see which would be stronger, and he said that the trash compactor bags were the strongest."

Coulson bought yellow latex gloves and borrowed Althaus' backpack.

"He said when he was running, he didn't want to carry any duffel bag. He wanted to be able to throw it over his shoulder, so he used my backpack, and he had a ski mask from when he was a little kid."

The night before the murders they bought the gas can. They filled it up at a Chevron station near the house.

"Bob suggested that we support our alibi by going to our farm, the farm that my grandfather owns, because there is no phone up there. And it's secluded, and there's no way to get into contact with anybody up there unless you actually drive up there."

"Now, we know that the murders happened on November the 13th, 1992. Was there any particular reason for selecting that day?" Rosenthal asked.

"The time change had already occurred, and that was one thing. Bob wanted it to be dark when he went into the house so no one could tell that it was him. And Friday the 13th was just a day that it happened, and the whole family would be there."

Coulson told him he wanted to wait until Sarah's baby was born.

"Let's talk specifically about—this began on the Wednesday before the murders. Did you and Bob Coulson go anyplace the Wednesday afternoon before the murders?"

"Yes, we did."

"Where was that?"

"We went to a neighborhood around the Coulsons. To scout around for a dark location where he could be dropped off and picked up."

They drove to San Marcos that same day. Althaus

wanted to break up with his girlfriend and Coulson wanted to see his uncle Peter.

"He wanted to talk to his uncle to make sure that he wasn't coming into town that following weekend," Althaus said.

"Now, you mentioned that there was a backpack. How was that backpack employed?"

"The backpack was to be used for Bob to store all of the zip cords, trash compactor bags, pistol, stun gun. . . . he took that to the house the day before and put it in the attic of his parents' garage."

Later that night, Coulson took the gas can to his parents' house.

"He told them that we had had it or I had had the gas can for a time now, and now—since we moved to our location on Glenmont, that it was smelling up the apartment and that we needed to get rid of it; and asked if we could store it at his parents' house."

Althaus left work early, at about 3:00 P.M., drove home and found Coulson with the groceries for the trip. Coulson was wearing shorts and a t-shirt, tennis shoes, casual clothes. He wanted the cameras at the apartment's exits to record him wearing casual clothes. He brought dark clothes with him and changed in the car. Althaus dropped him off approximately a block and a half from his parents'.

Althaus drove to the Exxon station at Jones Road and filled the car with gas.

"When you arrived at the pick-up point, was he there?"

"No, he was not."

Althaus circled three times before Coulson darted from the bushes. He crawled in and said, "Go, go, go."

He had the red gas can, he had a backpack and he had a crowbar.

"I asked him, 'What's the problem? What's the matter?' And he said, 'It went all wrong.' It didn't go the way he had planned it."

After he had thrown everything out the window as they drove, Coulson opened up to Althaus.

"What did he tell you he did first?" Rosenthal asked.

"He told me first that he had told his father that he had to talk to his mother about something, and he told his father not to come in the bedroom. Then he took his mother into the spare bedroom that his father had built."

"Was there any—did he tell her why he wanted her?"

"He just said he had something to tell her about the business that he wanted to go into, a surprise."

"What did he say happened?"

"He told me that he first tried to immobilize her with the use of the stun gun and that it didn't work. And she turned around and said, 'What are you doing?' "

"What did he tell you he answered at that point?"

"He said that he was in some money trouble and that he needed to take some things from the house and that he was just going to—he wasn't going to hurt anybody. That he was just going to tie them up and take some stuff and that he just needed some money."

"Did he indicate whether his mother struggled at all?"

"Yes. He said that she was the one that fought the most."

"Did he say how that struggle finally ended?"

"Yes. He ended up having to put a pillow over her face and smother her."

"After he said that he did that, did he tell you what else he did with respect to her body? Did he put a plastic bag—"

"Yes. He put the trash compactor bag over her head, zip-corded it and bound hands and feet and put duct tape around her mouth."

"Now, do you know if he had called the house before he had gone there that Friday to talk to his father or talk to his mother about anything that he needed to see them about that Friday night?"

"Yes. He said he had told them that he had some news about his business, and he needed to talk to them."

"Do you remember how long that was before the murder?"

"I would say the date of the murders."

Coulson killed his father next, Althaus testified.

"He said that his father was a wimp and that he was—easily took care of him."

Coulson next went into Sarah's bedroom and tried to use the stun gun on her, but it failed again. He tied her up and she asked repeatedly what he was doing. He needed money, nothing was going to happen. She asked why and he said, "Just because. Just because.' "

Sarah was tough and didn't put up a fight, he said. Coulson told her he was sorry and he loved her. He hugged her before putting the bag over her head. He was in Sarah's room when he heard Robin and Rick come in early.

"He said that he hurried and finished with Sarah and then closed the door. And he said by the time he got out there, Rick had already jimmied the screen door that he had locked, and they were already in the house."

Robin noticed the phone unplugged and plugged it

back in. It rang. She answered. It was Sarah's roommate, Dawn Ceyba.

When he couldn't separate Rick and Robin, he pulled out the pistol and told them to get on the ground. And then he told them that I was in the other room with a pistol on his mother and father, and that if they said anything or did anything that he was going to tell me to kill them.

He ran to the garage, picked up a crowbar and used it to hit Rick and Robin in the head.

"Why did he use the trash compactor bags?" Rosenthal asked.

"Bob's scenario was that he didn't actually kill anybody, and he wasn't going—he said he could live with himself if he did not actually kill somebody; if he put the bags over their head and they just all of a sudden died by themselves."

Once they died, he planned to take off all the zip cords and trash bags and put it in the backpack with him and then set the house on fire, pour gasoline all over the bodies and burn the whole house down. It would look like they had died of smoke inhalation.

"What did he say happened next?"

"He said that he had went around to pour gasoline all over the bodies, and in the process, the hot water heater had ignited the fumes from the gasoline."

The fire started where his father and mother were, and Coulson lit the rest with matches, Althaus said.

"Bob would constantly write things down on a piece of paper whenever we had conversations or either he would turn on the stereo real loud and whisper in my ear," Althaus testified. "He wrote down that half of $600,000 isn't bad."

"What did he do with the writings after he would make those writings?"

"He would go in the bathroom and burn them and flush them down the toilet."

"So I guess you didn't have any conversations there in the apartment then about facts of this case after it happened?"

"None whatsoever."

Althaus then detailed his actions over the next few days, including his meeting with the detectives in San Marcos and how he confessed to the crimes shortly afterwards.

Rosenthal asked him about meeting Bob at the motel.

"Basically, what was that conversation about?"

"It was basically a conversation to get Bob to admit to killing his parents and the Wentworths," Althaus explained.

"And did you say anything during the conversation about the fact that you did not actually kill his parents or you did not go inside the house?"

"Yes, I did."

Althaus told the court that a month before the murders Coulson decided to kill the whole family and not just his parents.

"He said that they didn't deserve any of the money, and if he was going to kill his parents, he might as well kill them all."

Their friendship began as a surprise to Althaus, who had feared Coulson in high school because he criticized him continually. Althaus enjoyed the favor he suddenly found from Coulson.

"Were you ever promised any specific money or any-thing like that to have participated in this crime?" Rosenthal asked.

"No."

"Bob promised that he would take care of me for as long as we lived together."

"Now, I guess the other thing I need to ask you, and I think I know the answer to this, too, but people have asked. Was there any sort of sexual relationship with you?"

"No, there was not."

Since Coulson was not working and Althaus was, Coulson took care of the apartment and fixed the meals.

"Was there any indications that he—where he talked about having access to boats or large craft?" Rosenthal asked.

"Yes. One day we were driving around, and we saw a boat, and Bob said, 'One day that will be ours.' "

"Okay. How about the apartment you were living in at the time the Coulsons were killed? Was it a—"

"It was a nice two-bedroom, 1200-square-foot town-home or high-rise, but that wasn't good enough. He wanted the penthouse."

"Did he talk about that?"

"Yes, he did."

"Did you have any discussions about taking trips together or having enough money to enjoy other things once the Coulsons were dead?"

"Yes, he did."

"He mentioned taking trips to Mexico or wherever we wanted to. We could do whatever we wanted to, whenever we wanted to."

"And how did that sit with you at that time?"

"At the time, it was great. He was—he was my leader, my protector."

"In the conversations y'all would have, I guess during these police shows and things like that, would you actually discuss the pros and cons of how to do different aspects of a crime like this?"

"Yes, we would."

"And realistically, did you participate in those discussions?"

"Yes, I did."

"Did he make suggestions or bounce suggestions off of you?"

"Yes."

"In fact, in—after one of those police shows, did the defendant make any comments to you about whether or not he expected the police would ever figure out who killed his family?"

"No. He said the police were stupid and that one day we would see this—the murders on *Unsolved Mysteries,*" Althaus answered.

"Did he indicate how far in the future that would be?"

"Years."

"He said that they'd never, ever figure it out. He said the police were too stupid."

"Now, during the time that you were having discussions with Bob Coulson in the car on the way to Caldwell, during the time you were at your apartment alone with him, any times after the murders, did—with the possible exception of the fact he said he might not have gone and done it initially—did the defendant ever express any remorse, any ill feelings about having killed his parents?''

"None whatsoever."

"Or his brother-in-law or his sisters?"

"No."

On cross-examination, Jim Skelton worked hard to poke holes in Althaus' story. Like all murder cases, his rested on conjuring up in the minds of the jurors enough reasonable doubt to earn an acquittal. Althaus was the key. Skelton labored to put questions in the jurors' minds about whether Althaus was the true murderer.

He began, "One thing I'm curious about: How many—seems like you've gone over this a number of times, the story you've now told the jury. Is that correct?"

"Yes, sir."

"As a matter of fact, if you will kind of help me.

"You're represented by a lawyer, are you not?"

"Yes, I am."

"And about how many times have you rehearsed and/or gone through this story with your lawyer?"

"With my lawyer none."

Skelton took pains to show Althaus was a liar, pointing out that he gave four different versions of his story to police. He spent half a day detailing the lies and fabrications of Jared Althaus.

"What you've done, as I understand it, you've worked out an agreement with the State that you're going to get twenty years out of this case. Isn't that true?"

"Correct. Twenty-year sentence."

Skelton asked why Althaus didn't go to someone he

trusted and tell them about Coulson's plans to kill his family.

"Bob would throw scenarios at me, yes, and I would put my two cents in worth because Bob—Bob took care of me. Bob made the beds, he did the laundry, he did everything, and so I idolized him."

"Because he made beds and did the laundry?"

"Because he was a figure that was dominating over me. He was—he had power over me."

"Do you realize you're telling the jury that you idolized a man who is talking about killing his entire family?" Skelton asked. "Now, this man that you consider your idol, did you ever say to him, 'Bob, you shouldn't be talking this way.' Did you ever try to talk him out of this?"

"The first time, I said, 'You're crazy. You're kidding.'"

Chuck Rosenthal called several Houston police officers who described at length the investigation of the Coulson murders: Brad Rudolph, who led Jared Althaus on the search for the items tossed from the car; John Swaim, who scared Althaus into confessing; and Jim Binford, who saw Coulson dance a gig after his family's memorial service.

Jason Althaus told his version of events, beginning with the trip to the farm. Defense attorneys tried to show that Jason had a clear reason for implicating Bob Coulson: saving his own brother. Because of Jared's testimony, he would not face the death penalty or even life in prison. Did he know that? Jason said he did, but had not been privy to discussions of the details of the deal. He testified with detachment, as if he and Jared, despite only a year's difference in their ages, were not particularly close.

Chapter Nineteen

As court-appointed attorneys, Bob Pelton and Jim Skelton had tried many high-profile cases in their careers. Some seemed hopeless from the start. Some people thought the Coulson case was one of them. But they saw a prosecution full of questions. No physical evidence tied the defendant to the murder. No one saw Bob Coulson in the area at the time. And Jared Althaus? He had made four different statements to the police. Who knew which was true?

They began offering their version of events on June 8th, a week and a half after the trial began. The audience and jury was attentive to the witnesses, folks who said Bob was a good kid, a churchgoing man who had never threatened anyone before. What everyone waited impatiently for was whether Coulson himself would testify.

Bob Coulson was a different type of defendant in Houston courtrooms. Not often does the legal system prosecute a child of some wealth, who had a good education and spoke articulately and earnestly. He could be charming and polite. Those traits afforded him a certain notoriety, and people crowded the courtroom to watch the drama unfold. One woman who had known him from a distance in high school attended the trial every day. Married with a six-year-old son, she helped the defense attorneys and sometimes would make third-party phone calls for Coulson so he could make long-distance calls from jail without calling collect.

Courtroom personnel didn't think too highly of Coulson. They wondered why the bailiffs allowed him to have visitors in a waiting room behind the courtroom during recesses. Once, the court reporter was in the room during one of the meetings. Someone needed to get something from the briefcase Coulson carried with him to court. He said the combination was 666. The reporter wondered if it was reference to the anti-Christ in the Bible's Book of Revelation. Court personnel nicknamed Coulson "Lizard Lips" because his lips were so thin they were barely noticeable.

On June 13th, Coulson took the stand. He walked to the stand looking like a young business executive headed for an important meeting in button-down collar shirt, red tie, navy blue blazer and slacks. His lawyer hit him immediately with the question everyone had wanted to hear him answer.

"Mr. Coulson, did you kill any member of your family?"

"No, sir. I absolutely did not," came the response, evenly and firmly.

"I want to go back with you, if you would, to what occurred on the date alleged in the indictment which is on, I believe, November 13th. I want you to go back with me on that day at this time," Skelton said.

He led Coulson through a series of questions about what his life was like then. Coulson recounted what the jury already knew. He was living in an apartment with Jared Althaus, whom he knew in high school but didn't become close with until the year his parents died. Mike Scott lived with them for a while, but moved out when he had money problems and felt like the "third man out."

"Did any problems develop between you and Jared?" Skelton asked.

"Yeah. Approximately—I would say it was probably within a month of moving in at the Glenmont location. Would have been about a month or two—month and a half, two months prior to November the thirteenth."

"What was your problem with Jared?"

"I started questioning as to what relationship he wanted with me other than friendship."

"Let me stop you here a moment. You've heard people characterize that Jared began to—for want of a better phrase—ape your personality or imitate your manner in doing things. Was this correct?"

"Yes, sir. I didn't notice that right away, but at [the] Perthshire address, I noticed that, and other people mentioned it to me, also."

Coulson said Mike Scott and Jerri Moore told him Jared had become like him, somewhat caustic.

"Would it be a fair characterization to say that you do at times have a caustic personality around people?"

"Yes, sir. Not always, but sometimes, yes, sir."

"What happened after that?"

"I got the impression that he wanted or would have—

would have liked some type of perhaps sexual relationship between the two of us as opposed to just a friendship that we had developed.''

Althaus had joked about homosexuality and called him ''honey.'' When they were cooking or doing dishes, Althaus would sometimes put his arm around Coulson. He would walk in on Coulson while he was showering, ostensibly to get toilet paper or toothpaste from the closet. Coulson testified he talked about his fears to his parents and to Sarah, the sister he said was his closest kin. He decided he wanted to move away from Althaus and looked at perhaps a dozen apartments, including the penthouse in a neighboring complex. When Coulson told Althaus he wanted to move out and that he had told his parents that, Althaus got mad and embarrassed. He begged Coulson not to move out and suggested they take a trip to hash things out. They would go to the farm on November 13th.

That morning, Althaus knocked on Coulson's door as he left for work about 6:30 A.M. Coulson said he went back to sleep for about an hour. About 9:00 A.M., he shopped for groceries for the trip at the Kroger supermarket behind their building. His friend Susan came over at eleven and stayed for about an hour, he testified.

After Jerri Moore cancelled their lunch, he stayed home until Althaus returned at about 3:15. P.M. They went down to load Jerri's car and handed some venison sausage to the maintenance man, Coulson said. They didn't take Althaus' car because it was too loud and ate gas. They drove out on I-10 to Town & Country Mall. Althaus told Coulson his mother had called and invited him to a family dinner at Luby's Cafeteria there.

Althaus was going to talk to a friend in the area while

the Coulsons ate. He would pick Coulson up at 6:00 P.M. Coulson walked over to the now-closed movie theater where he used to work. He said he was thinking about his first girlfriend, whom he met working there. He walked around the mall, and then went into the cafeteria. His parents never showed. Althaus drove up about 6:30 P.M., excited and sweating.

"Get in the car," he said, anxiously. Althaus had the windows open, despite the cold.

"Did he tell you why he was upset?" Skelton asked his client.

"He said he had an argument with this friend that he was—whoever this person was, this friend of his."

Althaus said he didn't want to talk about it. They drove into the night to Caldwell. He stopped the car several times to throw up on the side of the road, telling Coulson he had food poisoning. They arrived at 9:00 P.M., ate and then played cards. Althaus acted like his old self the next morning. Then Jason showed up.

"I was very—very upset," Coulson testified. "I stood up from where I was, but I don't recall the events that occurred after that."

On the trip back to Houston, Althaus said he was concerned because he had no alibi for the time the murders occurred.

"He said he was extremely scared and worried about going and talking to the police," Coulson said.

They made up the story of going to the farm at 3 o'clock.

"I was very afraid that they would just immediately say, 'well, since you don't have an alibi, we're going to put you number one on a list of suspects.'"

They went to the police station and were escorted

into different rooms. Coulson felt like the officer was looking him over.

"I felt like they were interrogating me, and I figured I was a suspect," he said, explaining why they lied to police.

"Could you tell the jury then your state of mind? Were you with it or what were you doing? How did you feel?" Skelton asked.

"I was fairly numb at the time. I was a little bit upset also because of the interrogation that I felt I had received from the police."

When they finally left the police station, Althaus was shaking and sweating, acting nervous, Coulson said. They went to his uncle Peter's motel room and Coulson signed papers allowing the cremations to take place. After about thirty minutes, Coulson and Althaus went home. Jerri Moore arrived at the apartment soon afterwards.

"I just didn't really want to see anybody," Coulson told the jury. "I asked Jared if he would mind, and he didn't say anything. He just went."

"Why didn't you want to see somebody?"

"I don't like getting upset in front of people and showing emotions or crying or anything like that. I've been that way since I was a small child."

Coulson said he went to church with his uncle Sunday morning and made no phone calls before he left. Overcome with emotion, he walked out of the church during the minister's sermon. Later that night, Coulson said, he went to dinner with Peter and the Emmotts. He felt numb as they discussed the circumstances of the estate.

"The only thing I remember is him mentioning Sarah's child being an heir," Coulson testified. "That's the only thing I recall from the whole entire conversation."

Skeleton handed Coulson a copy of his telephone bill from November 1992, and asked whether there were any calls to his cousin Linda Payne.

"Are there any records of a long-distance phone call being made to anywhere in Carolina on that particular day?"

"No, sir. There are none to South Carolina or North Carolina or to Tennessee, and that's where all my relatives live, in those three states."

"Did you call Linda Payne that Sunday evening?"

"Absolutely not."

"Did you have any discussions with anybody about Linda Payne coming into town?"

"Peter Coulson, my uncle, told me—I believe it was on Sunday at the lunch that we had—that they were coming into town. He said that she and Tim, her husband—I had never met him but I knew they had been married—were flying into Hobby Airport Monday. I think it was early afternoon."

The lawyer asked Coulson about Linda's relationship with his family. Coulson said he had not seen her for two years, when he saw her at his sister's wedding. Before that, he had only been around her maybe six times. She rarely came to Houston.

Bob Coulson was amiable on the stand, gesturing toward pieces of evidence, smiling. He appeared to be on an interview for a job.

"How would you characterize your relationship with Linda Payne? Were you a close friend of hers?"

"She was a cousin that I didn't get to see very often. I mean, we got along every time that I saw her, but I wouldn't—wouldn't characterize it as anything more than that."

Coulson told his uncle he would pick up Linda at the airport.

Skelton asked, "You heard her description of what transpired on the way in, and I believe she claimed you pulled down your eyelids and said, 'Look at the red,' or words to that effect. You sat in here and heard what she had to say."

"Yes, I heard."

"What's your recollection of what occurred in that conversation that you had with Linda Payne and her husband Tim Payne coming back from the airport?"

"We exchanged condolences when they got off the plane, I was introduced to Tim and got a big hug from Linda, and it just went normal from there to the time they—the last time I saw them on Tuesday."

Coulson said the first time he heard Linda make accusations against him was in court a few days earlier.

Continuing with his version of events, Coulson said he went by Jessica's [Guidry] house and then home after the viewing. He denied making an insensitive comment to Linda about the mourners. He woke with a start at 4:00 A.M. when the phone rang. It was Althaus. He was calling from a small town outside of Houston. He sounded upset and wanted to meet at a gym. Coulson dressed and went over there, but Althaus did not show up. He hurried home to dress for the funeral.

"Did you cry at the funeral?"

"Yes, sir."

"I cried beforehand in the—I don't know what you would call it—the area where they had the family prior to there and a little bit during the funeral, yes, sir. Some of it was during—actually up at the communion rail, not sitting down at the pew."

"Now, there's been testimony in which people described you've got your thumb and forefinger and kind of squeezed your nose. Do you recall doing anything like?"

"I don't think I squeezed my nose, but just rubbing like that."

Coulson acknowledged he walked his girlfriend to the car.

"Now, have you heard the police officer testify when you left Jerri at the car you did kind of a little dance jig is what he characterized that. Did that ever happen?"

"No, sir. That is ridiculous. I don't know what he's talking about."

Before Coulson left the church, his uncle told him they were going to meet at the house to gather some of the family belongings. He asked Coulson to come, too, to help locate things.

Coulson arrived after everyone else.

"Were these folks putting anything in boxes?" Skelton asked.

"I think they were just looking through things. I don't recall them putting things in boxes at that particular time in that room, no, sir. There wasn't a whole lot in that room besides—like I said, some bookshelves and the TV set. Things like that."

Linda was in the bedroom.

"What was she doing?"

"Rummaging through the drawers but mainly through the jewelry it looked like. The bed was not there."

Linda had testified she was sifting through the jewelry to separate the costume from the real.

"During this period of time that you were there, did any of the neighbors come by or any friends of yours come by?"

"Yes. Several of my friends—as we opened the garage door to try to fix the roof, several of my friends came over from across the street."

"Now, you heard Linda Payne testify that during the time you're at the house, you conducted a guided tour of where the bodies were located. Did that ever happen?"

"No, it did not. When I got there, like I said, they were in that back room, and when Andy and Daryl and Richard got there, the three of them along with somebody else—I believe Linda and Tim. I don't know if it was the whole group. You know, I don't know if Peter and everybody else was there or not. I don't recall. We went down into the other bedroom at the other end of the hall."

Peter Coulson arranged for everyone to go to a church member's house to divide the valuables for safekeeping. They sat on the floor and on the bed and passed jewelry and other items around, Coulson said.

"They would look at a picture and say, 'Well, this is a picture of whomever,' and give it, you know, to Peter if it was a member of our family, and if it was a member of the—you know, if it was like her mother or something like that, she would put it in a pile over here. Kind of sorting through things."

"And I think it was Linda who claims that during that time period you said you were going to trash, or words to that effect. I don't recall what. She did say something

about trashing all the family pictures or you're going
to throw them away or saying words to that effect.

"Did you ever say that about those photographs?"

"No, sir."

"I said that everybody should take whatever they
wanted, that we had plenty. Because we had a whole—
one of the closets at the house had numerous photo
albums, photographs, slides, you know, everything. And
the way—as meticulous as my father was, I was sure
we could get copies of anything we needed through
negatives or whatever."

Peter offered Coulson an expensive Minolta 35-
millimeter camera Otis bought the year before.

"I told him that I didn't know how to operate a
camera like that, that I'm a Polaroid kind of guy. I would
have no idea how to operate a camera like that, and I
knew that both Peter and Jack, both my uncles, were
camera buffs and I said, 'Y'all need them more than I
do.' And they both said, 'Well, we have that identical
model,' is what they—what they both said."

Bob Coulson denied saying he wanted to hock the
camcorder. He described all his dealings with Linda
Payne as cordial throughout the time they were
together. Neither Linda nor Tim expressed any concern
about anything he said or acted afraid of him.

He went home and stayed there until Althaus called
and asked him to come to the motel.

Referring to the tape made that night, Skelton asked
Coulson, "You've made numerous mentions about, 'Be
strong. They'll find out. Be strong'—of this nature—
'You're my boy. Stand beside me.' What are you talking
about?"

"I didn't want him to change the alibi story to tell them that we had lied."

"Why was that?"

"Because I figured if they found out we had lied, they would immediately suspect that we had committed the murders."

After he was arrested, police began questioning him.

"They were saying that Jared had said a whole bunch of things and, you know, said I had done this, that and the other. A lot of the time actually was spent with them talking to the guy in the front seat trying to locate where it was we were going and people trying to catch street names and things like that. I was actually helping them because they didn't—had no idea where they were at all."

"Now, you realize of course that the police's position is you admitted in the back of the van that you killed your family."

"I saw a quote that had been written down in the back of the van was to the essence that—"

"Did you make such a statement as that to the police?"

"No, I did not."

"And I believe there were words to the effect that: 'I had charged on my credit cards. There was no way out.' Words to that effect. Did you say that?"

"I told them I owed money on my credit cards, but I did not say that quote, no, sir."

"Did you make any admissions then about killing your family?"

"Absolutely not. No, sir."

Coulson explained that he hurt his knee and after surgery and the resulting brace came off, his doctor recommended he exercise. He said he started lifting weights and played tennis. But he couldn't work because he had to pick up water bottles weighing between forty-five and fifty pounds. He carried one hundred twenty to two hundred fifty a day, lifting them off the truck and carrying them and installing them in businesses.

His financial problems stemmed from the cut in his pay while he was on disability, he said. When working he was bringing in $500 a week, injured his income ranged from $200 to $400 a week.

Coulson explained he had been interested in buying Glasstronics, a windshield repair business, since 1989 or 1990. The company services car dealerships, truck rental companies, rent-a-car agencies, repairing windshields on site. He had worked for the company in Houston and wanted to buy it, but the owner was not interested in selling. Coulson went to San Antonio instead. He borrowed $3,000 from his parents, but came home a few months later. In March, he began negotiating with the Houston owner to buy his franchise for $20,000.

Coulson sought loans from banks and other financial institutions, but was turned down. He asked his father for help, but Otis refused. Instead, Otis said he would co-sign the loan if the seller would finance, Coulson testified. It would cost $5,000 more to do it that way.

"Did you get close to closing the deal?" Skelton asked.

"He said that was fine; that he would call me the next day. And he didn't call me, so I called him back the next day, and he said that a guy had come up with the cash, and he had just sold it, I guess, one of those two days."

"Now, there was testimony about you being angry or upset about this. Is that correct?"

"I was upset at Ken, yes."

"Were you ever upset with your father?"

"No. He had agreed to help me do that, to co-sign for me. I didn't have any reason to be mad at him."

Ken Smith was the first person Coulson had talked with after he was allowed to make a phone call from jail. It was Wednesday and he had been up since 4:30 A.M. Monday. He couldn't sleep in jail, he said, because of the noise and people harassing him.

Ken Smith, Skelton reminded the jury, had testified that Coulson had told him, "What the hell. I did it. I'm not going to run."

Coulson responded, "The leading up to it—obviously, like you said, the no sleep and the first phone call and all of that. As soon as we—I got through to him, I—I don't really know what I was expecting from him, you know, as his attitude or whatever, but it was, I would say, perhaps accusatory."

Coulson said he wasn't expecting that from someone he considered one of the people closest to him, a mix between a friend and a father. He was upset.

"I expected the Ken that I always knew, you know, to answer the phone and for us to have a conversation, but it did not . . . Like I said, after his first statement, it didn't go like that at all."

Smith asked him if he killed his family.

"I was fairly taken aback by that."

"What was your response?"

"I said, 'What the hell. If I did it, I'm not going to run,' is what I told him. Because he had mentioned— there were other things in the conversation before that about when the police had arrested me and things like that, you know. And he—he was basically asking—I mean, he pretty much came out and said it pretty directly. He was asking me if I was involved. That was quite a ways into the conversation. That wasn't the first thing he said. But I was very upset by that point in time, and I was very frustrated."

"What did you mean when?"

"When I said, 'What the hell. If I did it,' I was referring to was it going to matter as to him? Was he not going to be my friend? That's what I'm saying. I had that—my attitude had changed dramatically from what I expected him to be saying to me, and I was very upset by all of that. Because as good as friends as we were, I would have expected support from him pretty much under any circumstances, and that was totally not the case during that conversation. I didn't feel it was the case."

"Now, you heard Jerri's characterization of the conversation. And I believe, if I'm not mistaken, she admitted she was confrontational to some degree when she was talking to you," Skelton said referring to Bob's jailhouse visit with his girlfriend.

"Yeah. To say the least, yes."

"Was she angry when she was talking to you?"

"Very much."

"And did she tell you why she was angry?"

"I do not believe initially she told me, but from the first two or three questions, I had a pretty good idea."

"And that was why?"

"She asked if I had AIDS, had I ever stolen any money from her and I believe asked if I had taken people out in her car on dates or—"

"People or girls?"

"Girls."

Coulson acknowledged that he told Jerri Moore "All Jared did was drop me off and pick me up." But he said, his voice brimming with sincerity, he meant that Jared took him to the mall and picked him up. He said she also misconstrued his meaning when he talked about breaking their lunch date that Friday.

"Well, she had—one of the more accusatory things that she said—she said, 'I wish you would have been with me that weekend. Then you would have had an alibi,' is what she specifically said. 'Why didn't you?' I believe was the rest of that conversation. And that's when I made that comment. I said, 'If you hadn't broken lunch with me, it wouldn't have happened.' You know, I wouldn't have gone out of town with Jared. And she didn't question me about any of those statements either. She just went on and asked some things about if I had known Jared and—went to San Marcos, you know, during—prior to our arrest and things like that. She was quizzing me on a bunch of stuff like that. I guess some of that was in the paper. I don't know where she got that information."

Coulson said Jerri had visited him in jail 10 to 15 times and they talked on the phone a hundred or more times.

Skelton walked Coulson gingerly through the last week of his parents' lives. On Thursday, Coulson drove to his parents' house to pick up his birth certificate. He needed to send it with a form to the Social Security Department because of his disability.

Jurors listened as he recounted his friendships with Mike Scott and Scott Smith. He had met Scott Smith first, in junior high school. Mike had come along after they had entered high school. They had run around with others from the band, perhaps eight more.

"Now, during that period in high school, were there ever any jokes among that group or comments made among that group about—from you or other people about their parents dying and getting money and/or spending inheritances?"

"Yes, there was," Coulson said earnestly.

"And with that group—among that group of young people, whose family, at least from your kids' discussions, had money? I'm not talking about large amounts of money, but at least from kids' viewpoint, had some money."

"I would say at least three."

"And who would that be?"

"Myself."

"If I could stop you there. When you were in high school, did you have any earthly idea about what the Coulsons were worth?"

"During high school? No, I really didn't. Probably not until—I guess when I was in college which would have been right after high school."

The families of two girls probably had money, the rest were middle income.

"Now, were any comments made by you back in high school about spending inheritance or words to that effect?"

"I'm not sure if it was back in high school or not. Sometime either high school or thereafter, yes, there were. There were several occasions that I can remember specifically where things would occur that would bring up the comments. For instance, one time my parents—basically they lived in a—I guess you would call a middle-class home.—I believe in '88 they bought the Camry that I have discussed earlier in testimony."

"What was unusual about your folks buying a Camry?"

"They had bought several new cars before, and they were not your elegant cars by any means, I guess, to put it in a nice way. They weren't cheap, but they were not expensive by any means, and that was very odd at the time, that they went ahead and purchased the Camry. And when they did, it was just so out of the blue. One day, they had no discussion about it, and the next day, they bought it, as far as I knew. And I told—I believe Scott and there may have been other people around at the time. I don't recall specifically. I basically was fairly excited and told them that they—I think I put it, 'bought a real car.' I didn't mean that in any derogatory way but just—it had been an ongoing joke for a number of years because we owned Chevettes and cars along that line which is kind of the brunt of a lot of jokes amongst our friends about the kind of cars we owned. And I—everybody was fairly amazed that they had gone out and purchased this car, and at the time, it was— like I said, there were jokes for a number of years prior to that . . . and it just came up that—I don't even recall specifically if I was the one that said it—I don't even believe that I was—that, 'There they go spending the inheritance.' And everybody just laughed, and it wasn't a big deal. Nobody said they felt bad about it or anything like that."

Coulson admitted that as his parents were leaving on a trip to Europe in the 1980s, he had said to a friend, "Well, I guess if the plane crashes, I would be set." But he meant no ill will. He was simply referring to a joke his dad had made when he was going over the details of his will, insurance and other important papers with Robin shortly before the trip.

"My dad mentioned–since he had brought the wills out again, he had to go over all this because they were flying. He had mentioned—he didn't joke very often, but when he did, it was usually—everybody kind of stopped and looked at him because, you know, he didn't have that type of attitude usually. And he made a comment about, 'I want to go over this with y'all in case the plane were to crash,' or something like that is what he was telling us as we were going through the wills and just through emergency information, things like that."

Skelton moved on to discuss Coulson's personal life. He explained that he was adopted at age three, and had no recollection of either of his biological parents.

"Did you ever have to seek any type of counseling or psychiatric care or help because of any claim of trauma that happened to you from your natural mother and father?"

"Not to my knowledge, no, sir."

Skelton told the jury the defense lawyers had found Bob Coulson's natural mother and father.

"And when was the first time you saw your natural father again?"

"During jury selection. Maybe a month, a month and a half ago. I don't recall exactly when it was, but it was during jury selection."

The father had flown from his home in Rhode Island to Houston for the trial. The mother had met Bob a month before the trial began.

Coulson took his first job at sixteen, at Randalls, then worked in the mall, at a bakery, a child's clothing store. After high school, he attended one semester at Southwest Texas and the next at Houston Community College. He worked at UPS Truck Leasing, a division of UPS Delivery.

He was not jealous of Robin; the friction between them stemmed from rivalry. He considered Robin a brown-noser, making frequent visits to Mary's house to work on arts and crafts projects.

Chapter Twenty

Word spread quickly among the Houston legal community that Chuck Rosenthal would get a chance to cross-examine Bob Coulson. By the time the prosecuting attorney rose to begin his questioning the courtroom was packed with lawyers, anxious to see the longtime prosecutor square off with his foe. Rosenthal considered Bob Coulson the essence of evil.

"When the Lord handed out whatever it is that makes us feel empathy for others, Bob Coulson just didn't get it," Rosenthal said years later. "He killed his family like someone stepping on a cockroach."

Rosenthal had studied Coulson's life for months. The police report filled 200 pages, a wealth of dates, statements, and records. Only a sliver actually got into the court record. Rosenthal knew that Coulson often bragged about his sexual conquests and once had sex in front of a large picture window with a girl so everyone in her apartment complex could see what he was doing. Rosenthal wanted to nail this guy.

He began with, "Don't have any doubt—and you're not contesting that you are in fact Robert O. Coulson, are you?"

"No, I'm not," Coulson said, shifting slightly in his chair as if he were adjusting his mind for this new line of questioning. Rosenthal spit out a rapid-fire sequence of questions, ranging over just a few minutes from why Coulson borrowed money from ITT financial to Althaus' 4:00 A.M. call to how the police treated him after his arrest.

Coulson kept cool. Politely, completely, he answered each query.

"When did your parents install the burglar alarm in their house?"

"I believe we had it for probably two years, give or take."

"Did you know the code?"

"Yes, sir."

Rosenthal asked what was in the attic and then quickly moved to, "How did you feel about what you claim were sexual advances made toward you by Jared Althaus?"

"It bothered me very much."

"And were you repulsed by it?"

"That's probably a pretty good term, yes, sir."

"And you never did anything to invite those or make advances yourself?"

"No, sir, I did not."

He asked Coulson about the tape of his meeting with Althaus at the motel just before he was arrested.

"You heard yourself saying, 'Let me hold your hand. Put your arms around me. I love you.'"

"Because he was very nervous."

" 'I'm your boy' or 'I'm your man. I'm there for you.' Those kinds of things?"

"Yes, sir."

"And you didn't hear Mr. Althaus responding to those things, did you?"

"He didn't respond very much through much of the tape, I don't believe, no, sir."

Coulson denied having any sort of special hold on Althaus.

"He's his own man," he said.

"Are you testifying that you hadn't gotten him to the position where you could manipulate him into doing almost anything except go inside that house with you?"

"I don't think I manipulated him to do anything, sir."

"One of the things you have omitted in your story about the events that happened after the murders is the telephone call that you made to Jerri Sunday afternoon after the murders. Do you remember that telephone call?"

"On Sunday? I don't remember specifically, no, sir."

"Let me see if I can help you. She testified that you called her and basically read her the riot act for having talked to Althaus and that you said that it upset him and you wanted her to quit calling because it was making Althaus more and more upset. Do you remember that conversation with her?"

"I do not remember that, no, sir."

"So was she lying when she testified about that?"

"I did not say that. I said I don't remember the conversation."

"Well, you had learned as of—what?—noon on the

fourteenth, according to your statement, that five members of your family had been killed."

"Yes, sir."

"And you drive back to Houston, you talk to the police, and you don't ask them anything about the case? You just listen? You wait for them to tell you things?"

"That's not what I said. They told us some things when we got there. I asked a few questions, and they basically hustled us off in the little rooms because they wanted to question us. I even asked things also about where [was] the rest of my family, if they were in town, and they basically told me I didn't need to worry about any of that until they were done questioning me. And then at the end, when—I believe Mr. Achetee was the one that interviewed me—when he was done and we went to go do the fingerprints, that's when I specifically asked the man that was there some questions. I don't remember the guy's name."

"What did you ask him?"

"I asked him what had happened at the house."

Quizzed on whether he met up with someone he knew at the Town and Country Mall the night of the murders, Coulson said he ran into a man who he had played air hockey with years earlier. He couldn't recall his name but described him as 5'9", brown hair. Coulson used the guy's cellular phone to call his parents.

"But, of course, there would be some record of that call on a portable telephone, so you completely forgot who that person was, didn't you?"

"No, sir."

"Well, that never happened, did it?"

"Yes, sir, it did."

No one at Luby's Cafeteria, where Coulson said he

was to meet his parents, recognized pictures shown by the prosecution.

Coulson detailed the conditions his father had set down for making the loan for the windshield repair business. Otis had wanted insurance, a business plan, a meeting with the franchise owner and for his son to get out of debt.

"Which phone did you use to call Linda Payne on Sunday night, the fifteenth?"

"I did not call Linda Payne ever," Coulson responded.

Rosenthal then asked about family members.

"You didn't much care for Rick, did you?"

"I didn't really have any problems with him at all. He reminded me a lot of my father in a lot of ways, and I think that's why Robin liked him. He and I never had any problems."

"Well, you didn't like Rick because he was basically the son that you weren't to your mother, wasn't he?"

"No, sir. I don't believe so."

"He would come by and help her do things, he was gentle with her, he was kind to her when you weren't. Isn't that true?"

"No, sir. I don't believe that is true."

"Why did the family go out to eat?" Rosenthal asked, referring to the Friday night get-togethers. "They didn't used to go out to eat, did they?"

"No, sir. My mom used to cook basically every meal, and she had stopped I guess basically about the time most of us moved out, that being the kids. She wouldn't cook as much, and she would cook family type—fish and chicken which wasn't the favorite meal amongst the children. So when we would go out, generally we would go to one of five or six different restaurants.''

"Well, that's not why you stopped having meals at home, was it? You stopped having meals at home because you were always disruptive of the family there in the house, and they felt like if they went out, then you wouldn't be disruptive. Wasn't that the real reason that things changed?''

"No one ever said that to me, no."

"Wasn't that the same time your mother told you not to come by the house anymore unless you called first?''

"She had said that from the day I moved out."

After questioning Coulson about his disability payments, Rosenthal slipped in, "When did you buy the bags?''

"I never purchased any bags, sir."

"You never bought the trash compactor bags?''

"No, sir, I did not."

Coulson told the jury the wood furniture in his parents' house was special because it was made by his grandfather.

"So I assume then that when Jared Althaus testified that you said you were going to burn up the furniture because it would be worth more burned than salvaged that you never said that either?'' Rosenthal asked.

"No, I did not."

"So he's lied about that, too?''

"Yes, sir."

"Okay. And incidentally—just so we can get the record straight—when Linda Payne said that you did call her that night and that you were upset about several things, she's lying about that conversation?''

"Yes, sir. I did not call Linda Payne."

"And you're saying that Jack Emmott lied about the call that he says that you made to his home before church on the fifteenth?"

"About the phone call, yes, sir. I spoke to him at church, but I did not speak to him on the phone."

"So just so far, we've got Jared, we've got Linda, and we've got Jack Emmott all lying about you over this couple-day period. Is that correct?"

"Yes, sir."

As Bob Coulson finished his two days on the stand, Chuck Rosenthal wondered how the defendant had called Linda Payne in Summerville without creating a record of the call. Rosenthal had already pulled the phone bills for the house. No Summerville call was listed. He trusted Linda implicitly, so Coulson must be lying. After court, he called Jared Althaus.

"Did y'all have a long-distance service?" he asked.

Yes, came the response. Rosenthal said he wished they had the time to search for those records. Althaus replied there was no need. An organizer like Otis Coulson, Althaus had them in his files. He'd bring them over. Sure enough, a phone call to Summerville was there, just as Linda had described.

The next day in court, Rosenthal put the phone log in his inside suit coat pocket.

After Bob Coulson was seated again in the witness box, Chuck Rosenthal got right to the point.

"I think you've told us not—not once but several times yesterday that you absolutely did not make any telephone calls to any of your relatives on Sunday to talk to them about your parents' death or about any plans that they had had to come to Houston or anything like that."

"Yes, sir."

"And I also think that you told the jury yesterday that Jared Althaus had a telephone long-distance service that y'all had at the apartment there. Do you remember what the—

"Yes, sir."

"—what the name of that service was?"

"I believe it was Metro Media or LDS or something like that."

"Okay. And you're sure about the fact that you did not call Linda Payne on Sunday night to talk to her about coming to Houston?"

"Yes, sir. Our records show that I did not."

"No. I'm not talking about the records talking. I'm talking about your memory."

"Yes, sir. My memory—my recollection is that I did not."

"And you're as certain about that as you are certain you didn't go to your parents' house on the thirteenth and kill them?"

"Yes, sir. I did not kill my family."

"Mr. Coulson, let me show you what I've marked for identification purposes as State's Exhibit No. 110."

Rosenthal walked to the witness stand, faced away from the jury, and reached inside his coat for the phone record. He opened the coat just wide enough for Coulson to see the post-it note he had placed inside. It said, "Gotcha." He handed over the records and asked Coulson, "Do you recognize those records?"

"No, sir. I've never seen them before. Let me look at them real quick."

Coulson looked over the list, balanced and started to shake. The call was there.

"Okay. Now, when Jared Althaus got a Metro Media bill, you would basically pay your share of whatever long-distance calls you made, and he paid whatever long-distance calls he made. Right?"

"Whenever we got the Southwestern Bell statement or whatever list, the Metro Media charge is on it, yes, sir. And we would also pay a percentage of, you know, the monthly bill also; the $25, $30 for the hook-up."

"Okay. And your personal checkbook shows that you wrote several checks to Jared Althaus over the several months that y'all were living together, didn't it?"

"That I wrote to Jared?"

"Uh-huh."

"Probably so, yes, sir."

"Because basically what y'all did was you divided up the bills. You paid your share of the bills, and he paid his share of the bills?"

"Yes, sir."

"Now, I think Mr. Skelton had written down some numbers here." Rosenthal read a telephone number out loud for Coulson to verify. Then continued with, "And do you now remember making a call at 9:34 P.M. from that telephone to Summerville, South Carolina, area code 803, [number]?"

"No, sir. I do not remember making that call."

"Lasted nineteen minutes."

"I do not recall that. That's the first time I've seen any records to show that."

"Does State's Exhibit No. 110 refresh your recollection or memory about the calls you made on the fifteenth of—you know, November of 1992?"

"No, sir. I still do not recall."

"Well, these are the records for y'all's Metro Media charges, aren't they?"

"Does it show the phone number on that?"

Weakly Coulson sputtered, "I'm sorry. I'm saying if there was—what the phone number was. Like that. From the initial—from the house or from the—oh, okay. I'm sorry. I do not recall making those calls, no, sir."

The point was made. Bob Coulson lied. If he lied about something as unimportant as whether he called his cousin, he'd certainly lie about killing his parents and any number of other details in his story.

Rosenthal noticed, though, how swiftly Coulson recovered from the blow. As the questioning moved to other subjects, Coulson regained his image of the boy next door.

"Now, did you ever deny to the police officers that you killed your parents?" the prosecutor asked.

"No, sir. I didn't say anything."

"And you didn't make any kind of statements at all to them, I suppose?"

"I answered their questions about whether I owed money and how my knee was and things like that, yes, sir."

"As you testified before—Ken Smith misunderstood what you had to say about, 'What the hell. I did it.' ''

"Yes, sir."

"What was the conversation that led up to your making the statement to him about whatever—"

"I don't remember the whole conversation. He had started off by—I told him I had called Jerri first, I believe, and he made some mention as to—I believe he said he knew where she was, but, you know, he didn't say anything besides that about her. He was asking questions. I really do not remember the entire conversation.''

Rosenthal asked Coulson if he had shaken his head ''no'' when Jerri Moore asked him in her jailhouse visit if he had killed Sarah first.

''I believe that's right. I believe I put my hands on my head and just looked down, yes, sir.''

''Okay. You didn't deny killing Sarah. You just didn't—you just didn't say that—''

''I don't believe I made any reply at all whatsoever to that.''

''And then she asked you, 'Why did it happen?' And you said, 'Well, if you would have gone to lunch with me that day, I probably wouldn't have done it' or 'It probably wouldn't have happened' ''?

''No, sir. Before—just prior to her asking that question, she had asked about going out of town [together] was what she had brought up. That was what she had talked about just prior to me making that statement.''

''So, let me see if we can get this lineup right. You're saying that so far in this trial that Jack Emmott has lied, that Linda Payne has lied, that Tim Payne has lied, that Sergeant Jim Binford's lied, Jared has lied. How about Jason? Do you say he's lied, too, about the comment that said, that you were angry enough to kill your parents?''

''Yes, sir. I did not make that statement to him.''

''Okay. So Jason's lied. I guess we're anticipating that Bolk and Rudolph are going to lie and that Ken Smith and Jerri Moore are mistaken about things that you've said. Is that—''

''Yes, sir.''

Rosenthal asked where the Coulsons and Sarah were buried.

"I don't specifically know, but I was told Knoxville."

"When were they buried?"

"I do not know that either. My family was not talking to me, so I had no way of knowing."

Coulson was asked, "Won't you concede at least that if you didn't do it, no other one person could have done this?"

"I have no idea how many people did this, sir."

"I mean, because your parents certainly wouldn't have separated for a total stranger."

"I would have no idea, sir."

"And a total stranger wouldn't have known where that crowbar was in the garage."

"I have no idea if that crowbar was in the garage or not."

"You're the only person that stood to profit from their deaths, aren't you?"

"I was named in their will, yes, sir."

"Certainly you wouldn't want to do anything to hurt your parents. I mean, basically, they were people who took you in, who raised you when your own parents didn't want you. Is that correct?"

"Yes, sir. They adopted us, yes, sir."

"And you wouldn't want to do anything to hurt Robin and Rick. Robin was basically your only relative you knew of at that time, the only flesh and blood relative?"

"Yes, sir, she was."

"And Rick had never done anything unkind to you before in his life, had he?"

"No, sir. Not Rick."

"And you certainly didn't want to hurt Sarah because she was your favorite. She was the person who basically stood up for you when some of the other relatives down-played your value, didn't you?"

"I don't know about down-played my value, but yes, sir. We stood up—we took up for one another, yes, sir, on numerous occasions."

"She loved you when others got a little tired of you?"

"I don't know if anybody ever got tired of me, but she was there for me, yes, sir."

"How long did it take them to die, Mr. Coulson?"

"I didn't kill my family, Mr. Rosenthal."

"Did you notice in the autopsy report on Sarah the large gash on her thigh?"

"I have not seen an autopsy report, sir."

"Did she get that gash when she was thrashing around while she was trying to catch her breath?"

"I have not seen the autopsy report, sir."

"Was the idea to kill your folks to get the money to be able to move into Jerri's social status so you could be more accepted in the community, better financially off? Was that the idea?"

"I did not kill my family, Mr. Rosenthal."

"And of course, your family means so much to you that you don't really care anything about the money that you would inherit, do you?"

"No, sir."

"And the—I guess you don't have any—any—you wouldn't find anything wrong about saying that if the jury convicts you in this case, you would give up any right, title and interest to that money or give up any royalties that might be done from books or movies that might be made about this. You would give that all up because you're basically saying you didn't kill your parents, and you loved those folks more than—more than the money?"

"If they found me guilty or not guilty, I would be more than willing to do that, yes, sir."

"Willing to give up all that—all that money just to prove to the rest of society that you didn't have any reason to kill your parents?"

"I would sign something today if you would like."

"Did you feel more successful after you killed them?"

"I did not kill my family."

"Okay. While you were planning to kill your parents, did you also plan to dispose of Jared afterwards so that there wouldn't be any witnesses to this?"

"I didn't kill my family, and I made no plans for anything regarding killing anybody."

"You will admit you've had considerable time with not a whole lot to do other than think about what you're going to tell this jury, didn't you?"

"I've been in jail for nineteen months waiting to go to trial, yes, sir."

"While you were in jail, did you meet a man by the name of Troy Bolk, B-o-l-k?"

"I've met a lot of people, but that name doesn't ring a bell."

"Do you remember telling Mr. Bolk that they could never convict you because you got rid of all the evidence?"

"No, sir. I never told anybody or had any conversation like that."

"And that you were going to be a millionaire after you got out of jail on this case?"

"No, sir. That's ridiculous."

"Pass the witness," Rosenthal said.

After some follow-up questions by the defense and the prosecution, Skelton rested his case.

Chapter Twenty-One

On June 16th, the twelfth day of testimony in the Coulson case, the lawyers faced the most frightening part of a trial: turning it over to the jury. Lawyers usually plunge into trials confident in their facts and their law. The one uncertainty is the jury.

Defense attorney Robert Pelton stood before the jurors and said, "I know this has been a difficult time for all of you, and I know that all of you have searched your souls and searched your hearts to try to find out what the right answer is in this case.

"I know some of you have prayed. We talked about that when we first talked to you on *voir dire*. We talked about praying before we came up here, and I know there's at least two or three of you that said a prayer before you came up here today because you told us that you were going to do that when we first mentioned it.

"I said a prayer, too. I said a prayer and asked God

to help me say the things to you that are in my brain and the things that are in my mind and the things that are in my heart.

"Because oftentimes what happens when we get up to talk to people, we forget the things that we've been thinking about for the last three months, so I've asked God to help me say the things to you that are in my mind and that are in my heart. And I've asked God to help you and to be with each one of you as you make your decision today."

Pelton said the decision the jurors made may well be the most important of their lives. It would settle a man's future.

"What do you know about Bob Coulson? You know that he's twenty-six years old. You know that he's got relatives and family and friends in this courtroom today. You know that his natural parents are here today. You know that all these other spectators are here today to see what's going to happen to him, to try to solve this mystery. But the mystery can only be solved by you folks because y'all have—y'all have the heavy burden of solving the mystery.

He called the murders a "terrible, terrible tragedy" that no one took lightly. No one thought it was right.

"We know that it's caused grief for all these folks that are out here. We know that—Ms. Payne is the lady that I see there. She has a lot of grief. The Wentworths are on the next row. I know that they have grief."

Pelton reminded the jury that they must find his client guilty beyond a reasonable doubt and that the police had found no physical evidence to tie him to the case, despite hours of thorough research.

"No hair samples, no lint, nothing to connect Robert Coulson with these crimes."

Arson investigators could not tell how many people started the fires. No one had seen Coulson at the house that night. No neighbors or motorists on busy Westview.

"Nobody saw a man walking down the street carrying a gas can and carrying a crowbar and wearing a cap and wearing a sweater. Nobody saw him out there.

"There's nothing on any of those clothes tending to connect Bob Coulson to this crime.

"There's a lot of verbiage is what there is. There's a lot of words.

"The prosecution wants you to think that Bob Coulson is some sort of Jack the Ripper mass murderer. Well, did he just wake up one day and decide to become a mass murderer? Look at his school records. I know that some of you were looking at his school records. If a person is going to turn out to be the kind of person that they want you to think he is, there would be something in his background to show that. Look at his school records. There's nothing in there to indicate that he was going to do this. In fact, his principal, Mr. Meischen, came up here and said that he was a good kid and that he had never seen Bob be a violent person.

"Another thing that I thought was a little bit strange—think about this for a minute: If Bob Coulson had just killed five people and Jared Althaus was the only person that knew about it, what do you think somebody would do? If they have already killed five people, why not go ahead and kill another person? Why not go ahead and kill another person, especially a person like Jared? I mean, everybody that testified has told you what kind of person Jared Althaus is. He's an emotional person—he got upset when he would break up with his girlfriends. He was emotional, he was upset. He was crying.

"The other people that testified—the lady from the church, Ms. Neff. Barbara Neff knew Bob Coulson because he was an acolyte in church. He had been active in church. Now, somebody that's active in church, been an acolyte, attended church with his family, are they all of a sudden going to run out and kill people?"

Pelton reminded the jurors that Barbara Neff testified Bob Coulson loved his family, had never threatened them and was not violent.

"What reason would she have to come up here and lie?" he asked.

"It doesn't make sense that Bob Coulson would have gone there in that neighborhood and committed this crime. It doesn't make sense at all. If he would have done it, somebody would have seen him, but nobody saw him.

"He lived there nearly all his life. People knew him and could recognize him even wearing sunglasses and dark clothes. Bob knew the fire station was minutes away; the house would not burn to the ground.

"What do you know about Jared?" Pelton asked. "You know that Jared got a sweet deal from the prosecution. Why did the prosecution only offer him a twenty-year sentence if he testified? They have a carrot hanging out in front of him right now because he still hasn't come to court, as far as I know, to hear a plea of guilty. He's still out there wandering. How many lies did he tell?

"Nobody actually saw anything, even Jared who claims to have participated in this crime. The man who bought the stun gun, the man that bought the gas can, the man that bought the gloves and the man—he tried to say, I think, that Bob wrote a check for one of those items; either the tie-downs or the gloves. Look at Bob Coulson's checkbook and see if there's a check for Furrow's in there. I don't think you'll find one in there. I don't think you'll find one.

"Jared wants you to believe that Bob Coulson told him that he killed his family, and he wants you to believe that Bob Coulson killed his family by himself. Now, you heard what Jared Althaus had to say. He went into very specific detail about every person that was killed. Now, is his memory that good that he's going to remember all that?

"Every person that was killed, he went into specific detail, even about the conversations that he claimed Bob had had with his mother, with his dad, with Sarah, with Robin and with Richard. Went into great detail about the conversations that he had. Does that make sense? Could he have been telling you about the conversations that he was having with them as he was killing them?"

Pelton mocked the testimony that Coulson killed five people, including a 209-pound jailer and walked away without a scratch on him. He also questioned the prosecution's claim that Coulson killed his family for money,

"Do you think he's going to kill somebody because they are $3,000 behind on his payments? If having bad credit is a crime—there may be several people in this room that might have a serious problem."

He listed the friends who testified for Bob, from high school, from the neighborhood, from work, and said it was a shame the decision would be based on what people said and not clear-cut evidence.

"Now, there is a lot of tragedy in here. I understand that. There's tragedy for the Wentworths, there's tragedy for Linda Payne, and there's tragedy for Mr. Emmott. There's tragedy for Bob's biological mother and dad. It's a tragedy for all of them to find their kids after all these years and realize that one of them is dead, and the other one is on trial for capital murder. It's a tragedy for all these people.

"But what I'm asking you to do is don't let all this hoo-ha get you wrapped up. Don't let the news media intimidate you, don't let the audience intimidate you. Do what you know is right in your heart. And if you pray to God, ask God to help you make this decision— do what you think—think about this case, and do what you think is right in your heart."

Pelton finished by saying, "I'm asking you, if you believe in God, to ask God to help you make this decision, and I'm asking you to search in the innermost part of your heart and do the right thing, and I know that you will. God bless you."

Defense attorney Jim Skelton stood up, walked toward the jury and thanked them for their attention and their hard work.

"I think the thing that has been the most damaging to our side of the case—if you want to term it 'our side of the case'—and it's something that's real hard to illustrate to a juror. We sit every day as defense lawyers— and that's when you have enormous numbers of people come to the courthouse that you've known, that you've lived with, that you've cared for to testify against you.

"You've probably never had the experience of sitting

in the chair of a defendant having to rely upon people that you thought were friends during the time of your living—you probably have not had that experience."

The ever erudite Skelton gave a discourse on a John Stuart Mill book whose premise was that most of society's wrongs were committed by basically good people, people with good intentions, but bad ideas. Skelton said the book described the trials of Socrates, Jesus Christ and Joan of Arc, all of whom were wrongfully executed. Jesus, he said, was accused by one of his apostles.

"Why do people do that?" Skelton asked. "Why do they abandon people? Is it because people are bad or is it because they look back at the perception they themselves had?

"What I think has happened in this case is that a lot of people came to the conclusion when this case first happened that Bob Coulson was guilty of this crime. I think that conclusion was made immediately by the police department because the police department testified—or at least they indicated what had happened—that whoever entered the house did not make a visible, forcible entry. At least the door wasn't kicked in. That doesn't mean someone couldn't have come to the door and the door could have been opened and somebody could have been forced in by a handgun or otherwise. But there was no forced entry.

"The implication is that the family knew the killer. No valuables were missing, ruling out burglary as a motive. And only one man survived.

"What happened when this case began is that there was a mind-set then that Bob Coulson was obviously the one guilty of this crime. He was the only one to profit. And once that chain begins rolling, there's virtually nothing that one can do that's not interpreted as being suspicious, evil or onerous. I'll give you an example. Big issue was made that Bob Coulson never cried at the funeral, never cried at the wake or never cried during the services. I thought that was a bit ironical.

"You know by history that we lost Jackie Onassis this year. If you recall back to those funerals when John Kennedy died, one of the things—this whole country lauded and praised that she held up so well. She didn't cry, she didn't show emotion. She held up, and she was brave about it.

"Now, according to this theory or the State's theory of this case: If one does not do that—that means Jackie Onassis might have been the one that paid the so-called Guys in the Grass. You know, that's nonsense. That's total nonsense.

"The prosecution painted Bob Coulson as a man, adopted by a loving family that opened home and hearts to him, reared him, took care of him, then as a young man, murders them all in a horrible, grotesque way. Duct tape on their mouths, heads covered with bags. Then he shows no remorse.

"You don't all of a sudden wake up—because the crossword puzzle is complicated that day—and decide to kill five people. It just doesn't happen like that. . . . Doesn't make any sense. There had to be something. Either slap a cheerleader or do something in high school to indicate this sort of character. It simply was not there."

Skelton said the prosecution's idea for motive was shaky. The estate was not large enough to justify five deaths. If that was his nature, why didn't Bob marry

Jerri Moore and her six-figure income, build up the estate and kill her? It would only be one person.

"You don't have to kill your parents because he could make more—in two to three years, married to Jerri Moore, [than] he could have made in his entire estate. That never made any sense to me."

Jared Althaus' testimony was illogical as well, he said. One person walks alone into a house and kills five people.

"Here's what I thought was interesting about Jared's story, what always bothered me from the very beginning: Everything that they've recovered or everything that was used was bought by Jared Althaus. The gun that he claimed that was used in the house, the nine millimeter, who owned it? Jared owned it. The gas can, who bought it? Jared bought it. The stun gun he claimed was used, who bought it? Jared bought it. Who is the only person that we can prove that bought gas during that time frame was Jared Althaus from his own gas receipt. Because that cuts two ways they've never talked about. It establishes the time, but it also puts Jared doing what? Buying gasoline on the same day the murders occurred.

"Now, you're different than anybody else. You can't do the guessing that the police can do and the surmising that we can do because you took an oath, and that oath said that you would follow the law and you would read that jury charge and apply the evidence to it.

"If you do your duty after you read that jury charge and you follow that law, there can be but one verdict you can render, and that would be a verdict of not guilty. Thank you."

* * *

It was now time for the prosecution to speak. First the assistant district attorney, Jeannine Barr, reminded the jurors the state put up twenty-four witnesses, police officers, firemen, medical examiner, family members, friends, the defendant's girlfriend, and the co-defendant.

She said she looked at the autopsy reports and thought, "Why? Why are we here? And why do we have to look at that, and why did I feel like I needed to apologize to you when the medical examiner was on the stand for having to go through all of that? Why? We are here because he brought us here."

She turned and pointed at Coulson, sitting stonefaced between his attorneys.

"We're here because of him. Why? Because of his greed, his love of money. The only thing he probably loves more than money is himself. And you look at the degree of planning that he went through to pull this whole thing off, and it's been enough to make you sick."

Barr noted that the defense attorney talked about what a tragedy the deaths were to the family members, citing them by name.

"But you know who he left out? Bob. Never said it was a tragedy for Bob. Never saw any signs of remorse from Bob. Why? Because it's not a tragedy for him. That's exactly what he wanted. He got what he wanted. The only glitch is Jared talked. He didn't get away with it. He made a few little mistakes that you can see from the way that the evidence went down, and the biggest piece of evidence that the defense neglects to talk about over and over and over again is the tape."

She asked the jury to listen to it again, hear Coulson's calm, controlled voice trying to keep Jared from confessing.

"Innocent people don't need alibis. This story about them making an alibi because Jared needed one, that's crazy. Innocent people don't drive around an hour after they've heard their entire family has been wiped out and think of an alibi when they supposedly already had one because he was in the mall talking to some guy that had a cellular phone. That's absurd."

She said Bob Coulson had eighteen months to concoct a story that would jibe with the prosecution's case.

"This is a guy that thinks that he can fool everybody."

He controlled Jared and thought the police were stupid.

"He probably thinks you're stupid, too, thinks he can get by with all of this by telling you this story that he tells on the stand. He's just a liar. He's lied so much and so often that he's almost good at it, and that's frightening."

Barr pointed out that during the police investigation Bob never denied killing his family.

"He says he couldn't get a word in edgewise. Isn't that mind-boggling? You're accused of killing everybody in your family, and you can't get a word in edgewise to say, 'Hey, I didn't do it.' You couldn't keep any normal person quiet. You would be shouting from the rooftops, 'You've got the wrong person.' Not Bob Coulson. He wants you to buy that excuse, too. And I love the little dance jig at the funeral. That's, to me, the most telling piece of evidence. He doesn't think anybody can see him. Once again, he thinks he's got everybody fooled. He thinks he's got it in the bag."

She implored the jurors to use common sense.

"Nobody else would want to kill the Coulson family.

"It was Bob. He's a manipulator, a manipulator from the time he's old enough to know how, and he's trying to manipulate you. Think about this case—and I've thought about it a long time; everybody involved in it has. And it seems to me that the defendant has betrayed the most sacred trust that any of us have. He's betrayed the trust and the love of family. Please, don't let him manipulate you, and don't betray your oath. Rise to his challenge that no jury would ever convict him, and feel good about it. Thanks."

Then it was Chuck Rosenthal's turn. He said Bob accused everyone else of lying, but Bob was the only one shown to be a liar. The defense suggestion that Jared was the true killer was ludicrous. Why would he do it? He had nothing to gain. But he gained his friend's trust and devotion by going along with the plan.

He killed his family for the money and Robin and Rick had to go, too, so he would not have to share.

"This little family—this little family that was about to bring new life into this world, with all the hopes and expectations, they had to die to satisfy his greed."

Rosenthal cited Bob's questionable behavior. He could eat, sleep, carry on normally.

"This stuff doesn't bother him at all. The inappropriate behavior at the funeral as seen by Jack Emmott, as seen by Linda Payne, as seen by other people: His behavior is totally inconsistent with what a normal grieving person would do which points again to the fact of what happened."

Otis Coulson was expecting his son for a conversation about a business deal, Rosenthal said. The notes were waiting on his desk.

"And you kind of wonder what happened when he got there. Did he smile at his mom? Did he give her a hug when he got there? Why wasn't Mary Coulson listed in the indictment? Because evidence that the police find are a plastic bag on her head. He tells Jared Althaus, who tells us, that he smothered her with a pillow. Detectives say they didn't find a pillow in that room. We've got alleged manner and means of death, so we don't know what that is as well as we do with Rick and Robin Wentworth. The law says, too, that I only have to prove that he murdered two people. I obviously don't want to have to prove anything more than I have to prove."

An interesting twist, he said, was that Bob showed his friends where the bodies were.

"Now, he hasn't learned anything from the police. He doesn't go to the police and ask them what happened. He doesn't go to the police and say, you know, 'Am I in danger? Is there somebody else that is going to get me?' He knew where that body was. Does that mean anything to you?

"The prosecution is right that $600,000 is not a lot of money to kill for.

"But it's a lot of money to him. And they don't need it because his parents are useless.

"You heard Jared Althaus and the way he testified. He testified about a lot of embarrassing things to himself. He did a lot of stupid things, but he told you the truth."

The fact that Coulson used to go to church meant nothing, the lawyer said.

"Judas went to church. That doesn't make him anything special. That doesn't make him a non-killer just because he's been to church when his parents made him [go] several years before. And, you know, I asked the question of two or three different people—and I don't know if it means the same to you as it does to me, but how would you feel about someone killing their entire family and then taking communion at church? Doesn't that really mock God to you? But he doesn't care. He doesn't care. He's in it for himself.

"Y'all know what happened. Y'all know the truth about what happened. Y'all know he's guilty. I know you don't want to have to make that decision, but you took an oath to. Because that's what all the evidence points to, and that's what the law points to. Now, please, go do your duty. I pray for you, too, but I pray for justice. Thank you."

Judge Donald Shipley sent the jury out to decide Bob Coulson's fate.

It took them three hours to decide.

Guilty as charged.

Chapter Twenty-Two

Early morning court reconvened for the punishment phase. The jury that convicted Bob Coulson three days earlier would now decide whether he lived or died.

In Texas, the prosecution must show the defendant is a continuing threat to society, that he intended to kill his victims and that all evidence that would tend to mitigate his crimes was considered by the jury.

The prosecution put up no witnesses, offering all the evidence and testimony from the guilt phase as evidence that Bob Coulson deserved the death penalty.

For weeks spectators wondered about the couple from out of town constantly positioned in the hallway outside the courtroom. They had spent long periods with their faces pressed toward the window to the courtroom, watching as much of the proceedings as possible. The couple was Bob Coulson's biological parents, and people wondered whether they would testify during the penalty phase.

The defense team had traced them through old records on file at what once was the Nueces County welfare office. Once they learned Coulson's father's name, they located him at his shop in Rhode Island. He in turn put them in touch with Coulson's mother in North Carolina, where she had lived for a decade. They had divorced twenty years earlier.

Pudgy with large blue eyes and sandy-colored hair, Coulson's father had wondered for years what had happened to his children. The last time he had heard anything about them was when someone from the Texas welfare agency told him if he didn't hurry up and sign the release papers for his children they would miss being adopted by a lawyer. He said he had been made to feel a failure because he had no money to get them back. Moreover, he would further ruin their lives by missing the opportunity to become part of a wealthy family.

His wife had moved to Corpus Christi with her boyfriend and then abandoned the children at the welfare office.

For Linda Payne, seeing the biological parents answered many of her family's long-held questions. All they knew until then was that Robin and Bob had been taken by their mother to the welfare office. And now here she was face-to-face with these people. The parents and Linda did not speak, even though they spent large periods of time together in the courthouse hallway. When Bob Coulson testified, they had stood inches apart peering through the windows in the courtroom's double doors.

Hiding behind dark glasses, Coulson's biological

mother seemed confused and bewildered. Her flecked hair was closely cropped. She wore a flowered dress with little jewelry. Carrying a card of some sort to the stand, she was the defense's first witness. She seemed to read from the card occasionally.

"Would you tell the members of the jury how you're related to Bob Coulson?"

"I'm his biological mother," she said timidly.

She told the court she was from Rhode Island and was raised by her grandparents, who had never let her spend time with her mother. She saw her father only once or twice when she was a child.

Gently, Pelton asked, "Would you tell the members of the jury about some of the things that happened to you when you were a child?"

"I was molested by my grandfather all the time when I was little. I was beaten with a horsewhip every day. We never had anything. I never had Christmas or birthdays or nothing."

She met her former husband in the eleventh grade and they had married three years later. He had worked in a factory and later driven a cab. They had separated when he lost his job and money troubles mounted. She had worked any number of jobs, nurses aide, waitress, maid.

Living in an apartment with her children, she had met a man.

"We moved to Corpus Christi so he could finish— and he was in the Navy. And he just—he stayed there until he finished, and then he was going to go back to Oklahoma. But he had folks—he was adopted when he was little, and he didn't want his folks to know that he was going with a married woman or that she had children, so he left me. And when he got back in contact with me, it was either I would have to marry him and go on with him or, you know, do something with the children. And I just thought that if I gave them up, they would have a better life than what I did when I was little."

The lawyer asked if she and her former husband talked about the children.

"No, sir. You know, this wasn't anything that was planned or nothing, what I did. He was real good to the kids when they were with him and I. It was just that he didn't want his folks to know that I—you know, that I was married and had children."

He left her and went back to Oklahoma and she said she tried to make it work with the children but couldn't. She worked as a carhop.

"When I would go to the store to buy some bread or something for us, they would want a toy, and I couldn't afford to get it for them. So I decided myself that that would be the best thing for me to do."

She testified neither she nor her former husband abused the children.

"I loved the children," she said. She hoped someone would give them a better life.

"I just didn't have the money to take care of them," she said, weeping. "And I—he didn't—you know, I don't really think he wanted them."

She left Corpus Christi and went to Oklahoma to be with her boyfriend. She never saw her daughter again. Her son she saw when she visited him in jail a few months earlier.

She testified she changed her mind a few days after leaving the children and tried to get them back but the welfare officials would not let her have the children. She wrote four or five letters and called.

"What response did you get?"

"That I couldn't do it. They wouldn't let me have them back."

She said they gave her no reason.

"Did you finally give up on trying to get the kids back?"

"No, sir. I never gave up. I tried to find them all their lives, but I just had not had any luck."

She wrote to television shows, asking for help, but said they asked her for money. She never had money.

She thought about her kids every day of her life, she said. And for almost ten years she lived in Clute, Texas, just miles from Houston. There, she said, she was hospitalized for depression three or four times.

"Why do you think you had to go to that hospital down there and be under the care of a psychiatrist?"

"Because of everything that's happened in my life from the time I was little, growing up and thinking about the kids all the time and everything. It was just hard to deal with."

Until last year, she saw a psychiatrist weekly in North Carolina.

"Tell this jury: Why are your nerves shot? Why are you depressed?"

"Because of one thing. I've always wanted to find Robin and Bobby. I've just had a tough life the whole time I've been growing up and everything."

In April, Pelton had called her with the news of her children at her home in North Carolina, where she lived with her husband. She had one grown son with her second husband.

"How did you feel after I called you that night?"

"Happy and sad. I didn't—I couldn't sleep no more or anything. I just finally heard something I've always wanted to hear. Then I had to hear the bad part."

A few days later, she was reunited with her son.

Skelton said, "You know the predicament we're in now, don't you?

"Yes, sir."

"We're in pretty bad shape right now, aren't we?"

"Yes, we are."

"You understand they have found him guilty of killing your daughter, Robin?"

"Yes, sir."

"How does that make you feel?"

"Sad. But I know she's in a good place, and I'll see her some day."

The natural father came before the court next. At forty-seven he lived in the same town where he had grown up. His dad had been a policeman, his mom a homemaker. Both had died before he was eighteen. The next year he had married a seventeen-year-old schoolmate.

Pelton asked him why they had separated after five years of marriage.

"Well, it was mostly money problems. I had problems with her sister who was kind of interfering with the marriage. And I got hurt in my job a couple of times which—I'm sorry. I was falling behind in my bills and stuff, being out of work."

They were barely surviving and fought all the time.

"What did you try to do up there to get the kids back?"

"I got a letter from Corpus Christi saying that she

had left the kids off in Corpus Christi. And Rhode Island sent me a letter to go to a meeting in Rhode Island with the social workers; and I went to the social workers, and they wanted me to place the kids for adoption. And there was a big fight about it and stuff and whatever. They wanted to do this."

He tried unsuccessfully to get the $850 he needed to bring his children back to Rhode Island.

"I wanted to do what was best for the children, and I had signed—I signed the papers."

Pelton asked him how he felt about his son.

"I feel very good about him. I've had some very nice conversations with him. I feel he did not do this crime, and I do not wish to see him given the death penalty."

He and his son spent time together every day for the six weeks he had been in Houston.

"Are you willing to do anything that you can try to do to help your son?"

"Yes, I am."

Rosenthal passed on cross-examining Coulson's biological mother, but he wasn't going to let his father go.

"Did you look at the scene video, see what happened at the Coulson house, what handiwork your son had brought on the Coulsons?"

"No, I did not."

"What do you know about your daughter?"

"I know that she has been murdered."

"Do you know that she was a loving child who helped handicapped kids?"

"I believe that they both had been helping people throughout their lives."

"Robin's husband had a handicapped sister, and she helped take care of that girl, too."

"Yes. I was not aware of it."

"She was a sweet and kind lady—nobody has anything bad to say about Robin. She was just a wonderful lady."

"I'm glad to hear that."

"And your son killed her."

"Well, the jury has convicted him of—" Rosenthal had no further questions.

Leaving the courtroom, Coulson's father told reporters he hoped the jury would let his son live.

"I've lost him once. I don't want to lose him again," he said.

After six weeks in Texas, he and his former wife left the courthouse and flew back to their respective homes. The jury had not yet begun deliberating their son's fate.

The defense called others to tell about Bob Coulson's good side: his guidance counselor, the neighbor across the street from his parents, a church friend. They all said he was a good kid, went to church, never threatened anyone. He deserved to live.

In her closing argument, Jeannine Barr told the jury that the testimony from Coulson's natural parents was touching.

"The fact that he was placed for adoption is sad, but there are a lot of people that are put up for adoption, and when you think about it in the big picture, it was really a blessing. Look at what Mary and Otis Coulson did for him. They provided for him a loving family, a financially-stable family. They gave him opportunities, they wanted him to go to college. And what kind of thanks did they get for it?"

Anticipating the defense would raise the issue that

Coulson had never been in trouble before, Barr said, "Those things can also be turned into aggravating factors. Here's a guy that's had every break in life. Every break. From financial to loving support. Everything was there for him.

"Please don't forget the victims in this case. We've spent a lot of time talking about the defendant this, the defendant that, but don't forget Mary and Otis and Sarah and Rick and Robin.

"That's the true tragedy in this whole case: The defendant has single-handedly destroyed three generations of people. And I've got to tell you that if killing your own family for greed isn't enough to deserve the death penalty, I don't know what is. Thank you."

Jim Skelton pulled himself from his seat and set out a history lesson on Lincoln's assassination, when a doctor by the name of Mudd treated John Wilkes Booth and was castigated for it. He said he felt folks felt that way about Coulson.

"Because I've watched some of the jurors during the part of the time when the testimony was given, and I know when Robert had Bob's natural mother on the stand, when she was going through that tragic story, I don't know whether it was intentional or not, but I noticed one of the jurors kind of rolled her eyes back like, you know, 'Do we have to have listen to this? Really? Let's get on to the part of killing people.' At least that's the impression I got. Let me remind you of something: This has not been easy for any human being in this courtroom."

He said he wanted to share a concern.

"They're going to paint a picture to you of a horrible monster, a man without conscience, a man without remorse, a man who would kill five people for greed. Those sort of people are not born overnight. You don't go to sleep and one morning wake up, and you're a monster. Doesn't happen. There are always signs in people's life that lead to that. And, therefore, that second factor that we've talked about—which you should consider on punishment—that should assist you is somebody's background. Now, the reason we brought the mother and father up here was not for mitigation at all. The reason being: Sometimes people who have tragic backgrounds, who have gone through trauma as children, who have been traumatized, this will scar them for life. [They] may do acts of violence in the future. There's none of that here. I'm saying that the picture they paint to you is not consistent with what you've been told about this man's background.

"Bob Coulson is not a monster," Skelton said. "His biological parents tried to do what was right, his adoptive parents did, too. He had a normal home with typical teenage rebellion, nothing more.

"This evidence may be sufficient to make you comfortable with a guilty verdict, but is it sufficient to make you comfortable saying his life should be taken? Are you that comfortable with what you've heard in this courtroom?"

Bob Pelton wanted to talk from his heart. He had read the jury questionnaires the night before to try to remember the personal details of their lives. He called one juror by name and reminded him he had said he wanted to be sure someone was guilty before he could execute him. Another wanted to consider criminal record. Another wrote about God. He called juror after juror by name.

"You're not going to be sitting here with all these happy people and all these TV cameras and everything is just wonderful and fine. You're going to be by yourself somewhere. Some of you know what it's like to be alone and to have that lonely feeling in your heart. And you're going to be thinking about your life—it may be when you're laying on your deathbed. But when we face our maker, are we going to think: "Did I make a mistake?"

He asked the jury to look at the evidence, read Coulson's biological mother's letter, see for themselves why she was crying as she testified.

"They gave those children up once, and they've just now found them. They found their son. And I guarantee you—people say that he doesn't have any emotions. He does.

"Keep in mind, it's the same government—this government that wants you to kill Bob Coulson is—the same government [for which] you work about four months out of the year to pay income taxes. It's the same government that won't let you smoke in this courthouse."

Pelton appealed to their sensitivities, rubbed their guilt, tried to make them feel that the death penalty was immoral.

"Mr. Potts, how can you go preach on Sunday and tell those people up there, 'Well, you know, we voted to execute a man?' I don't see how you can do it. Honestly, I don't see."

The death penalty will not bring the Coulsons or the Wentworths back, he argued.

"What do you think Jesus would say to you if he was here?"

With a look of disgust on his face, Chuck Rosenthal stood up and said, "I usually don't comment on opposing counsel's argument, but the piousity in this room could be cut with a knife. He's telling you he's not trying to put any extra burden on you by singling you out by name and saying what you said in your jury questionnaire? Well, that's hogwash. What you're here for is to make decisions on what you knew up front was going to happen."

Rosenthal said there are two Bob Coulsons.

"There was the Bob who loved his sister Robin, and there was a Bob Coulson who wrapped a sack around her head, tied her up with duct tape and beat her with that crowbar.

"There are two Bob Coulsons, and it's the Bob Coulson who committed the murders of the Wentworths that we want you to sentence today. Mr. Pelton tells you that when Moses came down from the mountain with the tablet, it said, 'Thou shall not kill.' If you'll notice: Modern scholars have found what the word says is, 'Thou shall not murder.' And that's what he's done. He's committed a mortal sin. He has murdered five people. Five and a half people, actually. And one of the other commandments that he forgot to mention, conveniently, the only commandment with promise: 'Honor thy mother and father.'

"And the promise is that if you do that, you will be

able to live long on this earth. And he didn't honor his mother and father, and he's not going to be able to live long on this earth if I have anything to do with it.

"And I'll tell you what: Mr. Pelton also said the law doesn't deter anybody from committing crime. I can tell you that one person it has deterred is me. I went to that house, and I would kill him myself if the law didn't stand between me and him.

"And the government that he talked about, the government that's asking you to do this is the government that gave you this penal code and protects you from people like him. And the government that he talked about and tax dollars are paying for his defense. And the government that he talked about was the government that set up the laws that say, 'We can't find him guilty because we want to'."

Rosenthal told the jury Coulson had motive and planned the murders with precision. He could do it again. He lied when he didn't need to, about things that didn't matter. He bought his weapons in September to be ready for November murders, after Sarah's baby was born and the time changed. He set up his alibi. In his testimony, Coulson regularly made a distinction between something that was expensive and something that wasn't.

"You see, he has this twist on everything where he puts a monetary value on everything, and that motive was still in his heart last week when he testified.

"He was cold-blooded. Strangled then set his family on fire. And he set fire to a home in a residential neighborhood. No thought to any at all.

"He didn't care.

"He feels no remorse.

"Bob Coulson evidently lacks something that separates all of us from animals. What Bob Coulson lacks is compassion for other people. Bob Coulson cares only for himself.

"You're not God, but you all, as a body, can deliver us, can deliver all of us from evil, from the evil of that man right there. Thank you."

The jury talked and hashed out the case for five hours, before asking to retire for the night. It was after lunch the next day, June 22nd, when the jurors strode into the courtroom to deliver their verdict: Death. It would have been Mary Coulson's fifty-sixth birthday.

Epilogue

About a year after their daughter was murdered, Bertha and Richard McEver moved to Greenville, South Carolina, to be near their oldest grandson and his family. Bertha McEver was ninety. Unable to walk, she needed the full-time care of a nursing home. The grandchildren found an apartment for her husband nearby. With a quick wit and a sly smile, Bertha McEver was "Granny" to lots of people who were not her blood kin.

Usually willing to talk to just about anyone about anything, she did not talk about how her daughter, Mary, died. The McEvers shared everything through their long marriage, now in its sixth decade, but the subject of the Coulsons was off limits.

One spring day in 1994, her granddaughter, Linda Payne, came to visit. Granny was well aware of Linda's involvement in her daughter's estate and knew she had testified at the trial. In fact, Linda had addressed the jury on behalf of the family after they had sentenced her cousin to die by lethal injection.

"I need to tell you that you did the right thing," she had told the jurors, who wept and locked hands. "There is no doubt in my mind that Bob did this. I want to show you evidence that couldn't be brought in here like a gas can or a sweatshirt. For all of his life, Bob Coulson emotionally and mentally abused my aunt and uncle and family. And I know that and he knows that and now you know that. He made fun of them. He criticized them for giving money to their church. But my aunt wouldn't give up on him. She loved him to her death and she wouldn't have died if she hadn't loved him."

She then thanked the jury for what they had done.

"You've helped us," she had said. "We'll never be right. You'll never be right. But I know we'll be better."

Their action would help her family to stop hurting and start healing.

A short time before Linda addressed the jury and before he was sentenced to die, Bob Coulson talked with a television reporter. Sitting in a small office, the reporter asked him if he was a killer.

Coulson looked straight into the reporter's eyes and said emphatically, "No, sir, I am not." Then he smiled.

The trial left many questions unanswered, he said.

"The one that sticks out in my mind is who killed my family," he said. For many watching the broadcast, his tone was beyond strange. He asked, "Who killed my family?" as if he were asking when his shirts would be ready at the cleaners.

He also defended his lack of emotion, saying he keeps

his feelings in check. When the judge told him he would die for the crime, he stood straight and closed his eyes.

"You don't see me when I'm in my cell," he told the reporter, professing that he was "very bothered" about the deaths of his family.

Rosenthal said later he had never before felt happy to see the death penalty imposed until the moment he heard Judge Shipley sentence Bob Coulson.

"I've seen mean people in my life but he has to be one of the most evil people I've ever dealt with," Rosenthal said.

Coulson's natural father returned to his shop in Rhode Island and wrote to his long-lost son every three or four weeks. He visited him on death row one year for Bob's birthday.

"I honestly think his life was not all that bad with the Coulsons," he said a year after his son was convicted. "They probably gave them a much better life than we could have."

He said he remains convinced of his son's innocence.

"The only one who will ever know is Bob and he still says he didn't do it."

Moreover, he felt sure the sentence would be overturned on appeal. That was not to be. In late 1996, the Texas Court of Appeals upheld the conviction and sentence. Chuck Rosenthal estimated it would take two years before the final legal work was finished and Bob Coulson met death by lethal injection, a fate Jeannine Barr, the assistant prosecutor, once called far too civilized for him.

Bertha McEver knew her grandson was on death row at Huntsville, Texas, although she had not heard from him since his parents were killed.

Sitting in the warm spring sun of the nursing home sun room, Linda polished her grandmother's fingernails. Bertha McEver was a proud woman. In her youth, she had stood tall and straight and talked with a dignified air. She retained that stateliness into her 90s. Plus, she still liked to keep polish on her fingernails.

Small talk soon turned to big talk.

"Have you heard from Bob?" Bertha asked.

"No Granny, I haven't," Linda said. "Nobody's talked to him. I wish you'd quit thinking about him and worrying about him. He's how he is and he's never going to change."

"Those kids always had such a difficulty," Bertha said. "Mary always tried to love them so good and they never appreciated her."

"I know, Granny," Linda said.

"She wanted children so bad. She wanted more than one. She wanted a big family just like you all have. She did everything she could do for them. Robin had so many problems and I just don't understand how Bob had gotten so far gone, especially with Mary and Otis loving them so good. I just don't understand it."

Linda brushed a stroke of richly colored polish and smiled at her grandmother. No one can understand, she thought. It's way beyond that.

Her grandmother sighed and said, "I wish she had never taken those children."

WILLIAM H. LOVEJOY
YOUR TICKET TO A WORLD OF POLITICAL
INTRIGUE AND NONSTOP THRILLS. . . .

CHINA DOME   (0-7860-0111-9, $5.99/$6.99)

DELTA BLUE   (0-8217-3540-3, $4.50/$5.50)

RED RAIN   (0-7860-0230-1, $5.99/$6.99)

ULTRA DEEP   (0-8217-3694-9, $4.50/$5.50)

WHITE NIGHT   (0-8217-4587-5, $4.50/$5.50)

THE ONLY ALTERNATIVE IS ANNIHILATION ...
RICHARD P. HENRICK

SILENT WARRIORS   (8217-3026-6, $4.50/$5.50)
The Red Star, Russia's newest, most technologically advanced submarine, outclasses anything in the U.S. fleet. But when the captain opens his sealed orders 24 hours early, he's staggered to read that he's to spearhead a massive nuclear first strike against the Americans!

THE PHOENIX ODYSSEY   (0-8217-5016-X, $4.99/$5.99)
All communications to the *USS Phoenix* suddenly and mysteriously vanish. Even the urgent message from the president canceling the War Alert is not received, and in six short hours the *Phoenix* will unleash its nuclear arsenal against the Russian mainland. . . .

COUNTERFORCE   (0-8217-5116-6, $5.99/$6.99)
In the silent deep, the chase is on to save a world from destruction. A single Russian submarine moves on a silent and sinister course for the American shores. The men aboard the U.S.S. *Triton* must search for and destroy the Soviet killer submarine as an unsuspecting world race for the apocalypse.

CRY OF THE DEEP   (0-8217-5200-6, $5.99/$6.99)
With the Supreme leader of the Soviet Union dead the Kremlin is pointing a collective accusing finger towards the United States. The motherland wants revenge and unless the USS *Swordfish* can stop the Russian *Caspian*, the salvoes of World War Three are a mere heartbeat away!

BENEATH THE SILENT SEA   (0-8217-3167X, $4.50/$5.50)
The Red Dragon, Communist China's advanced ballistic missile-carrying submarine embarks on the most sinister mission in human history: to attack the U.S. and Soviet Union simultaneously. Soon, the Russian *Barkal*, with its planned attack on a single U.S. submarine, is about unwittingly to aid in the destruction of all mankind!

POLITICAL ESPIONAGE AND
HEART-STOPPING HORROR. . . .
NOVELS BY NOEL HYND

HORROR FROM HAUTALA

SHADES OF NIGHT   (0-8217-5097-6, $4.99)
Stalked by a madman, Lara DeSalvo is unaware that she is most in danger in the one place she thinks she is safe—home.

TWILIGHT TIME   (0-8217-4713-4, $4.99)
Jeff Wagner comes home for his sister's funeral and uncovers long-buried memories of childhood sexual abuse and murder.

DARK SILENCE   (0-8217-3923-9, $5.99)
Dianne Fraser fights for her family—and her sanity—against the evil forces that haunt an abandoned mill.

COLD WHISPER   (0-8217-3464-4, $5.95)
Tully can make Sarah's wishes come true, but Sarah lives in terror because Tully doesn't understand that some wishes aren't meant to come true.

LITTLE BROTHERS   (0-8217-4020-2, $4.50)
Kip saw the "little brothers" kill his mother five years ago. Now they have returned, and this time there will be no escape.

MOONBOG   (0-8217-3356-7, $4.95)
Someone—or some*thing*—is killing the children in the little town of Holland, Maine.

THE MYSTERIES OF MARY ROBERTS RINEHART

THE AFTER HOUSE   (0-8217-4246-6, $3.99/$4.99)

THE CIRCULAR STAIRCASE   (0-8217-3528-4, $3.95/$4.95)

THE DOOR   (0-8217-3526-8, $3.95/$4.95)

THE FRIGHTENED WIFE   (0-8217-3494-6, $3.95/$4.95)

A LIGHT IN THE WINDOW   (0-8217-4021-0, $3.99/$4.99)

THE STATE VS.   (0-8217-2412-6, $3.50/$4.50)
ELINOR NORTON

THE SWIMMING POOL   (0-8217-3679-5, $3.95/$4.95)

THE WALL   (0-8217-4017-2, $3.99/$4.99)

THE WINDOW AT THE WHITE CAT
      (0-8217-4246-9, $3.99/$4.99)

THREE COMPLETE NOVELS: THE BAT, THE HAUNTED
LADY, THE YELLOW ROOM
      (0-8217-114-4, $13.00/$16.00)

*Available wherever paperbacks are sold, or order direct from the
Publisher. Send cover price plus 50¢ per copy for mailing and
handling to Penguin USA, P.O. Box 999, c/o Dept. 17109,
Bergenfield, NJ 07621. Residents of New York and Tennessee
must include sales tax. DO NOT SEND CASH.*